THE
LITTLE
BOOK
OF
DORSET

DAVID HILLIAM

Other books by David Hilliam published by The History Press

Kings, Queens, Bones & Bastards

Monarchs, Murders & Mistresses

Crown, Orb & Sceptre

A Salisbury Miscellany

Winchester Curiosities

Why Do Shepherds Need A Bush?

First published 2010

The History Press
The Mill, Brimscombe Port
Stroud, Gloucestershire, GL5 2QG
www.thehistorypress.co.uk

Reprinted 2011, 2012, 2016, 2017

British Library Cataloguing in Publication Data.
A catalogue record for this book is available from the British Library.

ISBN 978 0 7524 5704 8

Typesetting and origination by The History Press
Printed and bound by TJ International, Padstow, Cornwall

CONTENTS

AUTHOR'S NOTE

Following the county boundary changes of 1974, Dorset was enlarged to incorporate a part of Hampshire, including Christchurch and Bournemouth. This book treats the new area as if it had always been a part of Dorset.

INTRODUCTION

The Little Book of Dorset is just what the title implies – nothing pretentious, and certainly not claiming to be a comprehensive history or guide. It is a somewhat quirky collection of some of the things that make Dorset unique as a county – the 'Wessex' of Thomas Hardy's vivid novels.

Dorset has had a fascinating past, going back to Jurassic times. It has been the centre of many crucial moments of English history and it has had associations with a huge variety of people, from Alfred the Great to Lawrence of Arabia and Enid Blyton.

Even in the twenty-first century Dorset remains the county of *Tess of the D'Urbervilles, The Mayor of Casterbridge* and *Far From the Madding Crowd*. It is the beautiful and somewhat melancholy world of Thomas Hardy, whose brooding presence is for ever to be seen in his memorable statue in Dorchester. Flowers still appear there on the anniversaries of his birth and death.

But also, alongside this, the Dorset of the twenty-first century is the scene of the 2012 Olympics, the vibrant nightlife of Bournemouth, and the many tourist attractions such as Bovington Tank Museum, Monkey World and Poole's arts centre, now called 'Lighthouse', where superb performances by the Bournemouth Symphony Orchestra can be heard.

It is to be hoped that readers of *The Little Book of Dorset* will want to visit and revisit this beautiful county again and again.

David Hilliam, 2010

PLACE-NAMES & PUBS

No other English county has towns and villages with so many magically poetic place-names as Dorset. John Betjeman recognised this when he began one of his poems by simply listing some of them: 'Rime Intrinsica, Fontmell Magna, Sturminster Newton and Melbury Bubb.'

THE TOP TWENTY
CURIOUS PLACE-NAMES IN DORSET

There are over three hundred towns and villages in Dorset – many with names which are intriguing and puzzling. Here are the top twenty place-names in Dorset which cause most surprise.

Affpuddle
Like many Dorset villages, Affpuddle is named after the River Piddle. It means 'the land by the River Piddle which belongs to Aeffa' – Aeffa being one of the early Saxon settlers here. In some place-names, the Piddle is somewhat prudishly changed to 'Puddle' to avoid bringing a blush to sensitive cheeks!

Bishop's Caundle
Several Dorset villages have 'Caundle' in their names: **Purse Caundle**, **Stourton Caundle**, and **Caundle Marsh**. They are situated near hills, and it is thought that 'caundle' was an ancient British word for a chain of hills. The 'Bishop' of Bishop's Caundle is the Bishop of Salisbury, who owned the manor here. 'Purse' of Purse Caundle is probably derived from a family name.

Blandford Forum
'The market town where there is a ford at which gudgeon or blay (Old English blaege) are to be found.' 'Forum' is the Latin word for a marketplace, and interestingly, in 1288 the town's name is recorded as 'Cheping Blaneford.' – cēping being an Old English word for a market.

Broadwindsor

The meaning of 'Windsor' in this name is the same as that of **Windsor** in Berkshire, from which the present royal family chose to be called. Literally, 'windsor' means 'river-bank with a windlass' – from windels, Old English for 'windlass', and ora, Latin for a river-bank. The original windlass must have been used for loading and unloading boats on the river. As for the 'Broad' part, this simply distinguishes the place from nearby **Littlewindsor**.

Chaldon Herring

'Chaldon' means 'hill where calves graze' – from two Old English words: cealf, 'calf', and dun, 'a hill'. Like so many other double-barrelled place-names, the second part (Herring) points to a family who owned an estate here, in this case, the Harangs. Their name is also found in **Herrison**, **Langton Herring**, and **Winterborne Herringston**.

Child Okeford

There are two other Okefords in Dorset – **Okeford Fitzpaine** and **Shilling Okeford** (more usually called **Shillingstone**). 'Okeford' itself is self-explanatory – 'ford by an oak-tree' – but the 'Child' in Child Okeford is not so easily explained. The Old English word cild meant 'son of a royal or noble family' – but who is being referred to is not known. 'Fitzpaine' refers to a previous landowner. Also, 'Shillingstone' derives from a surname – it is Schelin's 'tun' or hamlet.

Corfe Mullen

'Corfe' comes from an Old English word meaning 'cutting, or pass' – that is, a cutting between two hills. The same name occurs, of course, in **Corfe Castle**. As for 'Mullen', this refers to the mill which used to be here. The French word Moulin, 'mill' – as in Moulin Rouge – springs to mind, though the can-can is rarely seen in Corfe Mullen.

Fifehead Magdalen

'Fifehead' is a slight distortion of 'five hides' – where a 'hide' meant the amount of land considered sufficient to support one family. In the Domesday Book this estate was called Fifhide. 'Magdalen' refers to the dedication of the church here, to St Mary Magdalen.

Gussage All Saints

'Gussage' comes from two Old English words: gyse, 'water suddenly breaking forth', and sīc, meaning 'water-course'. As in so many double-barrelled village names, 'All Saints' refers to the dedication of the church. There are also two other 'Gussages' in Dorset, both with church dedications: **Gussage St Andrew** and **Gussage St Michael.**

Hazelbury Bryan

The 'hazel wood' on the estate of the Bryene family, who derived their name from Brienne in France.

Lytchett Matravers

The first part of this name derives from the Celtic Lētocēto, which means 'grey wood' – and this is probably the same as the first part of the name of Lichfield. The second part derived from the family of Hugh Maltravers, who owned the manor in 1086, the year of the Domesday Book. The same family gave its name to **Langton Matravers.**

Melbury Bubb

This village gains the second part of its name from the Bubbe family, who owned land and property here in the thirteenth century. William Bubbe held the manor here in 1212 – three years before the signing of Magna Carta. The first part, 'Melbury', means 'multicoloured hill.' The other Melburys in this area are **Melbury Abbas**, which belonged to the Abbess of Shafesbury; **Melbury Osmund**, which is probably named after 'William the son of Osmund' who is mentioned as having owned the manor here in the twelfth century; and **Melbury Sampford**, named after the Sampford family. Interestingly, in the Middle Ages Melbury Sampford had the name of 'Melbury Turberville' – after an earlier owner (with a name much more familiar to readers of Hardy!).

Minterne Magna

Perhaps surprisingly, yet so obvious, the 'Mint' part of the name actually refers to the herb, mint. The name Minterne, therefore, means 'the house where mint grows', with the second part of Minterne deriving from the Old English word ærn, meaning 'house'. As for 'Magna' this is the Latin word for 'large' and so distinguishes Minterne Magna from Minterne Parva ('little').

Old Harry

No, not a village, but a very distinctive sea-stack of chalk, rising out of the sea just off the cliffs at Studland. 'Old Harry' was another name for the Devil. In 1896 another sea-stack, Old Harry's Wife, collapsed into the sea.

Piddletrenthide

One of the many villages deriving their names from the River Piddle. This extraordinary name means 'Estate on the River Piddle assessed at thirty hides' – i.e. it could support thirty families (see Fifehead Magdalen earlier). The word trente is simply the French for 'thirty'. Sometime during the Middle Ages this village was referred to as 'Pidelthirtihide' – which perhaps makes its meaning clearer.

Ryme Intrinseca

This is the name that John Betjeman used to begin his poem on Dorset – but oddly enough he misspelt it! The 'Ryme' part is simply the modern word 'rim', and means that the place is on the edge or border of a ridge or perhaps a county boundary. The word intrinseca is Latin, meaning that it is 'within the bounds' – as distinguished from its opposite, extrinseca. There used to be a manor called Ryme Extrinseca in Long Bredy, but this has disappeared.

Sixpenny Handley

A fascinating name, which is sometimes even seen as '6d Handley'! 'Handley' derives from two Old English words, hēah and lēah, meaning 'high wood' or 'clearing'. The 'Sixpenny' part, which is more intriguing, means 'hill of the Saxons' deriving from an Old English word, Seaxe, and a Celtic word, penn, meaning 'hill'.

Toller Porcorum

A wonderful name, meaning 'Toller of the pigs' – as opposed to **Toller Fratrum,** a nearby village, which means 'Toller of the brothers'. Both porcorum and fratrum are Latin; Toller Porcorum got its name because of the herds of swine which were bred there, and Toller Fratrum gained its name from the fact that the manor used to belong to the Knights Hospitallers – who were 'brothers' in arms. As for 'Toller', this was once the name of the river which runs nearby. This is now renamed the River Hooke. Toller Porcorum was called Swyne Tolre in the Middle Ages.

Tolpuddle
Another name coming from the River Piddle. The first part – 'Tol' – is interesting because it records the fact that a lady called Tola used to own the lands here. In fact this lady was the widow of Urc, a 'housecarl' or bodyguard of Edward the Confessor. Urc was probably a part of King Edward's bodyguard. Tola generously gave all these lands to Abbotsbury Abbey a few years before the Norman invasion.

Winterborne Came
There are many 'Winterbornes' in Dorset, which are explained below, but the 'Came' part of this name is curious, because it is a corruption of Caen in Normandy. After the Norman conquest the manor here belonged to the abbey of St Stephen at Caen.

WINTERBORNES

There are two rivers in Dorset with the name Winterborne – which means a 'stream flowing in winter' – i.e. when there is more water to flow into them. The South Winterborne is a tributary of the River Frome, and the more northerly Winterborne is a tributary of the River Stour. On the South Winterborne river are many villages:

Winterborne Abbas – 'Abbas' meaning 'belonging to the Abbey (of Cerne)'.

Winterborne Stapleton – 'Steepleton' meaning 'village with a church steeple' (only three medieval Dorset churches had steeples).

Winterborne St Martin – named after the dedication of its church – an alternative name for this village is **Martinstown**.

Winterborne Monkton – 'Monkton' meaning 'village of the monks' – because the place formerly belonged to a French priory.

Winterborne Herringston – 'Herringston' named after the Harang family, as also in **Chaldon Herring** (see earlier reference).

Winterborne Came – see above for an explanation of 'Came'.

There are even more Winterborne village names on the north Winterborne river:

Winterborne Houghton – 'land on the Winterborne river owned by Hugh' – who probably was Hugh de Boscherbert, who owned property here at the time of the Domesday Book.

Winterborne Stickland – 'Stickland' meaning 'with a steep lane'.

Winterborne Clenston – 'Clenston' referring to the Clench family, who owned property here in the Middle Ages.

Winterborne Whitechurch – 'Whitechurch' is fairly self-explanatory, but it may be that it referred to the fact that the church was built of stone rather than wood.

Winterborne Kingston – 'Kingston' meaning 'farm or estate belonging to the King' – equivalent to 'Regis' as found in other names.

Winterborne Muston – 'Muston' meaning 'farm or estate belonging to the de Musters family' who owned property here.

Winterborne Tomson – 'farm or estate belonging to someone called Thomas', but in fact no one knows who this Thomas was. This 'Winterborne' consists merely of a church, a farm, and a seventeenth-century cottage.

TARRANTS

Similar to the Winterbourne rivers, the **River Tarrant** gives rise to eight village names along its length. The name 'Tarrant' is Celtic, and possibly meant 'the trespasser' because of its habit of flooding and 'trespassing' on the fields beside it.

Tarrant Crawford – 'Crawford' meaning 'a ford where there are crows'.

Tarrant Gunville – 'Gunville' refers to the Gundeville family who owned property here in the Middle Ages.

Tarrant Hinton – 'Hinton' meaning 'town or place belonging to monks or nuns' from the Old English word hiwan. Here, the nuns referred to were those of Shaftesbury Abbey, who owned the manor here.

Tarrant Keynston – 'Keynston' refers to the Cahaignes family, who owned property here in the Middle Ages.

Tarrant Launceston – 'Launceston' derives from the name of an individual or family, but it is not clear who they were.

Tarrant Monkton – 'Estate belong to the monks' – in this case the manor belonged to the priory of Cranborne and the abbey of Tewkesbury.

Tarrant Rawston – 'Rawston' probably means 'Ralph's farm or estate'.

Tarrant Rushton – 'Rushton' meaning 'land or estate held by the de Rusceaus family', who owned it in the Middle Ages.

MORE DORSET PLACE-NAMES

Shitterton
Found in Bere Regis, it is now called Sitterton on the current Ordnance Survey map – presumably for the same reason that Piddle has been bowdlerised into Puddle. The meaning of the original 'Shitterton' was that it was 'a farm at the stream used as a sewer'. (See Dorset's Naughty Names, p. 8.)

St Aldhelm's Head
Some old maps and books call this Dorset headland between Swanage and Weymouth 'St Alban's Head' – and indeed the Ordnance Survey Map gives both names. But as all Dorset folk know, St Aldhelm was Sherborne's first bishop, so much loved and respected that everyone knew him as a saint. St Alban had nothing at all to do with Dorset!

Brandy Bay
Looking towards St Aldhelm's Head, Brandy Bay is a shameless reminder that smugglers used it for landing their illegal barrels.

God's Blessing Lane
This curious name can be found at Colehill, north-west of Wimborne. The story behind it is that Oliver Cromwell billeted his troops near here before the battle for Corfe Castle. His men were 'blessed' here, to ensure victory.

DORSET'S NAUGHTY NAMES

Shitterton
Originally named for its drains, Shitterton was coyly renamed Sitterton in the Victorian age. However, in our more robust twenty-first century it has now proudly reasserted its older, more earthy, version – Shitterton. Predictably, Shitterton's wooden signboards were constantly being stolen by thieves with a lavatorial sense of humour. Shitterton villagers therefore responded by clubbing together, each paying £20 to purchase a large, engraved block of Purbeck stone weighing more than a ton and which is now firmly concreted into the ground.

Scratchy Bottom

A cliff-top valley between Durdle Door and Swyre Head, its odd name refers to the fact that is it a rough hollow. Famously, it was the scene of the opening of the 1967 film *Far from the Madding Crowd*, when Gabriel Oak's sheep were driven over the cliff-edge by his sheepdog.

Burnt Bottom

Thomas Hardy gave it the more dignified name of Norcombe. It is near Hooke.

Happy Bottom

A much more comfortable-sounding name, it is near Corfe Mullen.

Aunt Mary's Bottom

A Site of Special Scientific Interest, being a valley mire lying on the northern flank of Rampisham Hill. Sadly, no one now knows who Aunt Mary was.

Shaggs

A village near Bovington. Prince Harry, while stationed at the army camp in Bovington, rented a nearby cottage at Shaggs, allegedly sharing it with his girlfriend. Not surprisingly, his fellow-officers were much amused.

Pulham Down

Near Sherborne, it is believed by some to have a double-entendre, though this may well elude those of a pure mind.

Sandy Balls

Alas, it cannot be mentioned here as it is just over the border in Hampshire. It is a popular holiday centre near Fordingbridge.

SOME INTERESTING PUBS

The Bottle Inn, Marshwood

Nowadays 'The Bottle' is famous for hosting the Annual World Nettle-Eating Championship (see page 95) but it has existed since 1760 at least, and gains its name from being the first inn locally to sell beer by the bottle.

The building in the car park has been used as a school and then as a shop – selling, as the pub-owner boasted, 'everything from a mousetrap to a car'. When challenged, he obligingly sold the enquirer a mousetrap and a Rover 100.

The Damory Oak, Blandford

Just on the outskirts of Blandford, the Damory Oak pub is named after a famous tree that grew nearby. It was probably the biggest oak tree ever to grow in England. The statistics of this gigantic oak are staggering: it measured no less than 68ft round (20.72m) at ground level, and it was 23ft (7m) in diameter. It was reckoned to have been at its best in the fourteenth century, but by the seventeenth century it had become so hollow that twenty men could get inside the cavity, which measured 15ft wide (4.72m). At one time, an old man sold ale in it. Then, after the great fire of Blandford in 1731, two homeless families lived for a while inside the hollow trunk.

Sadly, the tree was sold in 1755 for £14, and was chopped up for firewood. The Damory Oak pub is the only memorial to this incredible tree. 'Damory' derives from the name of the D'Amorie family, who were given lands here by William the Conqueror – and Damorys still live in Dorset almost 1,000 years later.

The Quiet Woman, Halstock

For centuries this was a well-known coaching inn or pub, but it is now an excellent guest-house named Quiet Woman House, offering top-quality bed and breakfast accommodation. The 'Quiet Woman' was St Juthwara, or Judith, a medieval saint who had been beheaded – hence her quietness! (See page 156 for her story.)

The Smith's Arms, Godmanstone

Dorset boasts that this is the smallest pub in England. At one time it was a blacksmith's, and the story goes that King Charles II (reigned 1660–85) while visiting the area, drew up there to have one of his horses shod.

He asked for a glass of ale, and when the blacksmith told the king he had no licence, Charles immediately granted him one. It's a curious and picturesque pub, very tiny, with a conical-shaped thatched roof.

The Mermaid Inn, Portland

Local legend tells how a mermaid was washed ashore near here in the eighteenth century – and this is how the pub got its name. There are many stories of weird creatures coming out of the sea here. The sixteenth-century historian Raphael Holinshed described one such oddity:

> 'In the moneth of November 1457, in the Ile of Portland not far from the town of Weymouth was seen a cocke coming out of the sea having a great creast upon its head and a red beard and legs half a yard long: he stood on the water and crowed foure times and everie time he turned him about and beckened with his head toward the north the south and the west, and was of colour like a fesant and when he had crowed three times he vanished awaie.'

The King's Arms, Dorchester

A splendid old coaching inn situated in High East Street, built in about 1720. King George III would change horses here on the way to his holidays in Weymouth. Famous people who have stayed here include Princess (later Queen) Victoria, Edward VII (incognito), Lord Nelson, Augustus John and the Russian ballerina Pavlova.

For readers of Hardy's novels, this is the inn where Michael Henchard did his business in *The Mayor of Casterbridge*. Hardy himself knew this pub well, and described it exactly, not even changing its name:

> The building . . . was the chief hotel in Casterbridge – namely, the King's Arms. A spacious bow-window projected into the street over the main portico, and from the open sashes came the babble of voices, the jingle of glasses, and the drawing of corks.
>
> *The Mayor of Casterbridge*, Chapter V.

The Fox, Ansty

Not for nothing did Egon Ronay choose The Fox at Ansty as his first Pub of the Year in 1980 – and it has remained one of his favourites ever since. It was once the imposing residence of the Woodhouse family, famous for their brewing, and now its reputation for excellent food and drink draws countless 'foodies' from far and wide. Most notable, in every nook and cranny, is its unique and fascinating collection of Toby mugs – over 800 of them at the last count.

The Black Dog, Weymouth
This pub got its name because the master of a Newfoundland trading vessel gave the landlord a black dog from that country – a black Labrador. It was the first of the breed to be introduced into England.

The Antelope, Dorchester
Sadly, this is no longer a pub, but a part of a tiny, attractive shopping mall, and the Oak Room – a part of the original old Antelope Inn – is now a busy restaurant. But the Oak Room has a hugely important past, because it was there, in 1685, that Judge Jeffreys condemned 300 men to death or transportation in the 'Bloody Assizes' for taking part in the Monmouth rebellion.

St Peter's Finger, Lytchett Minster
This is the only pub in the entire country with this strange name. But the 'finger' is really a corruption of the Latin ad vincula, meaning 'in chains'. St Peter was often shown in medieval paintings as a prisoner.

Opposite this pub in the early nineteenth century was an important depot for the button-makers to bring their products to sell to the Case Brothers, whose grandfather had originally set up this industry in Dorset.

ARISTOCRATIC DORSET PUB NAMES

Several pubs in Dorset are named after well-known landowning families of the county: **The Drax Arms** in Bere Regis has the splendid coat of arms of the Drax family of Charborough Park for its inn sign. **The Bankes Armes Country Inn** at Studland and **The Bankes Armes Hotel** at Corfe Castle take their name from the owners of Kingston Lacy. **The Weld Arms** at Lulworth refers to the famous family who own Lulworth Castle. Other aristocratic pubs are **The Rivers Arms** at Cheselbourne, Dorchester, the picturesque **Hambro Arms** at Milton Abbas, and **The Digby Tap** in Sherborne.

FARMS AND FIELDS

In the eighteenth century, a wealthy and eccentric landowner named Thomas Hollis bought a large estate in Halstock and Corscombe. He was a passionate defender of liberty and free-thinking and set about renaming the farms on his newly purchased land, calling them after his heroes and even after abstract ideas.

Not only was there a Liberty Farm, but also farms called Neville, Locke, Sydney and Marvell. Hollis had close links with America, where he had made many bequests to universities, especially Harvard, where today there is a Hollis Hall.

Thanks to Thomas Hollis there are farms and fields in this part of Dorset which have American names such as Boston and Massachusetts. More oddly, there are fields named Toleration, Constitution, Education, Lay-preacher, Government, Understanding, Comprehension and Reasonableness.

There was even a Stuart Coppice – named for the grim reason that the hazel trees there had to be frequently beheaded!

2

BONES & BURIALS

The churches and churchyards of Dorset contain some surprises – and there are some odd tales to tell.

THE CURIOUS CASE OF THE CARNIVOROUS CAT

When Thomas Hardy died in 1928, his reputation as a writer was so great that nothing short of a burial in Westminster Abbey was deemed appropriate. Unfortunately, Hardy himself wanted to be buried in Stinsford, beside the Dorset church where he had worshipped since childhood. A somewhat gruesome compromise was agreed – his body would go to the abbey, but his heart would be buried in Stinsford.

Going about this odd business, the local doctor went to Max Gate to cut out Hardy's heart, and then left it on the kitchen table, wrapped up in a cloth. Shortly afterwards, when the undertaker

arrived to take possession of the 87-year-old heart, he was appalled to find that it had disappeared, and a cat was nearby, obviously having just enjoyed an unusual meal.

According to credible sources, the undertaker acted swiftly, with commendable presence of mind. He killed the cat and took it away with – presumably – Hardy's heart inside it. An amateur photograph of Hardy's funeral at Stinsford shows the clergyman bearing Hardy's heart in a wooden casket, rather larger than would be necessary to hold a heart, but of a convenient size to hold a cat.

KINGLY BONES KEPT IN A CUTLERY BOX

The bones of the Saxon fifteen-year-old king Edward (reigned 975–8) were buried in Shaftesbury Abbey, but the nuns there hid them at the time of the Dissolution of the Monasteries by Henry VIII.

The bones were then completely lost for almost 400 years. When they were finally rediscovered, they became the subject of a legal tussle between two brothers over who owned them. While the lawyers wrangled, King Edward's bones were kept in a cutlery box in the vaults of the Midland Bank (now the HSBC) in Woking, Surrey.

Eventually, King Edward's bones were given to a sect of the Russian Orthodox Church, and are now venerated by monks in a special shrine in Brookwood Cemetery, also in Surrey.

BONES MOVED FROM ST PANCRAS TO BOURNEMOUTH

Visitors to Bournemouth may be surprised to find that the churchyard of St Peter's, in the centre of the town, has the graves of William Godwin (1756–1836), his wife Mary Wollstonecraft Godwin (1759–97), together with their daughter Mary Wollstonecraft Shelley (1797–1851), the author of *Frankenstein*.

Mary Wollstonecraft was a champion of the rights of women, and her book *A Vindication of the Rights of Woman* caused consternation by advocating the equality of men and women. Horace Walpole called her a 'hyena in petticoats' for her views.

Mary Shelley had asked to be buried near her parents, who had been buried at Old St Pancras church in London. Accordingly, the bones of the Godwins were brought to Bournemouth by Mary Shelley's son, who had settled there with his mother.

A POET'S HEART

The poet Shelley was drowned off the coast of Italy in 1822, just a month before his thirtieth birthday. His body was cremated on the sea-shore, but his heart was snatched from the fire and was kept by his wife, Mary, for the rest of her life.

After her death it was found among her belongings wrapped up in a sheet of Shelley's poem 'Adonais'. Shelley's heart was later buried with their son, Sir Percy Florence Shelley, who lived in Boscombe and was buried with his mother's remains in St Peter's churchyard, Bournemouth. There is a fine memorial to the poet in Christchurch Priory.

PAROCHIAL NIMBYISM

'Lawrence of Arabia' – Thomas Edward Lawrence, *aka* Aircraftman John Hume Ross and *aka* Private Thomas Edward Shaw – was killed in a motorbike accident riding at speed in a Dorset lane. He is buried in the churchyard at Moreton, near his cottage at Clouds Hill.

His cottage is in the parish of Turners Puddle. However, neither the parish priest at Moreton nor the priest at Turners Puddle wanted his memorial – so the Bishop of Salisbury suggested that his life-size effigy should be placed in St Martin's church at Wareham, where it is now to be seen. In the true sense, this is a 'cenotaph' – in other words, an empty tomb.

DORSET'S ROLE IN THE ARRIVAL OF THE BLACK DEATH

The Black Death of 1348–9 resulted in the extermination of about one-third of the entire population of England. It's difficult to pin down an exact figure, but it's likely that the death-toll throughout the country was around one and a half million people – and it all started in Dorset, or more precisely Melcombe Regis, now a part of Weymouth.

Melcombe Regis was a busy and important port during the Middle Ages, where ships were constantly coming and going to France. It so happened that in July of 1348 a sailor or a passenger from the continent brought the dreaded bubonic plague to England. A medieval chronicler describes the sinister event: 'In this year 1348, in Melcombe, in the country of Dorset, a little before the Feast of St John the Baptist, two ships, one of them from Bristol, came alongside. One of the sailors had brought with him from Gascony the seeds of the terrible pestilence and, through him, the men of that town of Melcombe were the first in England to be infected.'

SIX INTERESTING PEOPLE BURIED IN DORSET

Mary Anning (1799–1847)
While still a twelve-year-old schoolgirl, Mary Anning discovered the first ichthyosaurus, and she went on to find many other dinosaur remains on Dorset's Jurassic Coast. Dinosaurs were unknown until Mary Anning's persistent search for the bones which are still so plentiful along Dorset's beaches. She virtually 'invented' dinosaurs. Mary Anning is buried at St Michael's Church, Lyme Regis, where there is a memorial window to her. Her father taught her to use a chisel to prise bones out of the cliffs.

Sir Robin Day (1923–2000)
Robin Day's modest tombstone can be found in the churchyard of St Candida and the Holy Cross at Whitchurch Canonicorum. Those who remember the television of the 1960s and '70s will instantly recall his genially forensic interviewing technique. Always polite, wearing a bow-tie, he pioneered the aggressive, no-nonsense questioning of politicians and public figures we take for granted nowadays with exponents such as John Humphrys

and Jeremy Paxman. He was a passionate advocate of televising parliament – indeed, perhaps parliament on TV is his most lasting memorial. With wry humour, his tombstone reads: *In loving memory of SIR ROBIN DAY, THE GRAND INQUISITOR.*

Cecil Day-Lewis (1904–72)

Visitors to Stinsford church, to see Thomas Hardy's grave in the churchyard there, may well be surprised to see the gravestone of another poet – Cecil Day-Lewis – just a few yards away from that of Hardy. Day-Lewis, who was appointed Poet Laureate in 1968 in succession to John Masefield, was such a fervent admirer of Hardy's poetry that he asked to be buried near him. The inscription on his gravestone reads:

> Shall I be gone long?
> For ever and a day
> To whom there belong?
> Ask the stone to say
> Ask my song

James Hammett (1811–91)

The story of the Tolpuddle Martyrs is told elsewhere in this book. When these Dorset labourers returned to England after their terrible experiences in Australia, they all sought their fortunes elsewhere in the world, except James Hammett. He stayed behind in Tolpuddle, and is the only member of the group to be buried in England. Hammett is buried in the churchyard of St John the Evangelist in Tolpuddle. The inscription on his gravestone, which was carved by Eric Gill, reads:

> TOLPUDDLE MARTYR
> PIONEER OF TRADES
> UNIONISM. CHAMPION
> OF FREEDOM

Richard Poore (d. 1237)

Unless you know Salisbury well, you are unlikely to know who Richard Poore was, but he was arguably the most important Bishop of Salisbury in all its history, for he designed and built the city of New Sarum completely from scratch in 1220, taking his clergy and all his flock down from the ancient hill fort of Old Sarum to build a new cathedral and a newly designed city in the valley below – the

Salisbury we know today. After his work in Salisbury he became an important Bishop of Durham, where he added new features to the great cathedral there. Then, on retirement, he came to be buried in the little Dorset village where he was born – in the little church of St Mary's in Tarrant Crawford.

Alfred Russel Wallace (1823–1913)

Alfred Wallace is famous for his work on evolution and his researches were carried on at the very same time that Charles Darwin was preparing his monumental book, *On the Origin of Species.* It was one of the great coincidences of history, and when Darwin realised that Wallace was about to publish his findings, he quickly decided to bring out his own book first – in November 1859. Alfred Wallace is buried in the cemetery at Broadstone, between Bournemouth and Poole.

Sir Francis Edward Younghusband (1863–1942)

Francis Younghusband led an amazing life as an explorer in Asia, crossing the Gobi Desert and travelling in India and Tibet at a time when these regions were virtually unknown. He was also a mystic, and has been called a 'premature hippy' – believing in cosmic rays, extra-terrestrial beings and free love. He was elected President of the Royal Geographical Society, and did much to encourage climbers to tackle Mount Everest. One of his domestic servants was Gladys Aylward, who became a missionary in China, and whose life was portrayed by Ingrid Bergman in *The Inn of the Sixth Happiness.* Francis Younghusband is buried in the parish churchyard at Lytchett Minster.

The ashes of **H.G.Wells** (1866–1946) were cast into the sea near Old Harry Rocks.

The ashes of **Dr Marie Stopes** (1880–1958), pioneer of family planning among other exploits, were cast into the sea off Portland Bill.

SOME DORSET EPITAPHS

In the churchyard of St Gregory's, Marnhull, is an epitaph of comfort to smokers. It is in memory of John Warren, parish clerk, and his wife. John died aged 81 in 1698.

Here under this stone
lie Ruth and Old John,
who smoked all his life,
and so did his wife.
And now there's no doubt
but their pipes are both out.
Be it said without joke,
that life is but smoke;
Tho' you live to fourscore,
'Tis a whiff, and no more

In St Martin's, Lillington, on a gravestone on the floor at the entrance to the aisle which once belonged to the Cole family, is this excruciating epitaph punning on the name Cole:

Reader, you have within this grave,
a COLE rak'd up in dust;
His courteous fate saw it was late
And that to bed he must;
So all was swept up to be kept,
Alive until the day
The trump should blow it up and show
The Cole but sleeping lay.
Then do not doubt, the COLE'S not out,
Tho' it in ashes lies;
The little spark, now in the dark,
Will like the Phoenix rise

In the church of St John the Baptist in Buckhorn Weston is a curious memorial stone in the chancel to a former rector who apparently had a curious hobby.

John Sampson, Rector, here doth rest in Christ
Divine, physician, anagrammatist,
He was baptised May 12, 1626
He died June 18, 1715, aged 90 years
Buried June 22, 1715

In the churchyard of St Nicholas, Worth Matravers, is a headstone to a little-known pioneer who successfully experimented with vaccination well before Edward Jenner, who has gained all the fame, credit, and a special medal from Napoleon Bonaparte.

> Sacred to the memory of BENJAMIN JESTY
> of Downshay, who departed this life April
> 16th, 1816, aged 80 years. He was born at
> Yetminster in this county, and was an
> upright, honest man; particularly noted for
> having been the first person (known) that
> introduced the cow-pox by inoculation, and
> who from his strength of mind made the
> experiment from the cow on his wife and
> two sons in the year 1774.

In the north aisle of St Michael's, Stinsford, the church in which Thomas Hardy attended for many years, is a memorial containing an interesting and curious name. Here is the first part of it:

> Near this place are interred
> AUDLEY GREY, esq and MARGARET his wife,
> He was the second son of Angel Grey,
> of Kingston Marleward and Bridport
> in the county, esq.

The interesting name in question is 'Angel' grey. Anyone who has read *Tess of the D'Urbervilles* will instantly remember Angel Clare – a name so unusual that one critical reviewer of *Tess* complained that for a man to be called 'Angel' was quite ridiculous.

MRS PERKINS ORDERS HER COFFIN TO HAVE A HINGED LID

Close to Christchurch Priory, just beyond the east end, in the grounds beside the river walk, is an astonishingly puzzling building. It intrigues those who walk by, as there is no indication as to what it is.

In fact it is a mausoleum which once held the body of a Mrs Perkins, a local lady who died in 1783. She had been terrified of being buried alive, so she gave strict instructions that her coffin should have a hinged lid. She wanted to be able to push it open if she suddenly woke up after her funeral. She also ordered that she should lie in a building with a special lock to its door that could only be opened from the *inside*.

Imagining every awkward possibility, she even stipulated that the building should be near the school which used St Michael's Loft in the Priory Church – guessing that the kids there would hear her shouts if ever she should get out of the coffin but be unable to get out of the building!

She died twenty years before her husband, and when eventually he died, her body was taken to be buried with his in the family vault. The mausoleum was then taken down and re-erected in its present position. It's now empty – but there are speculations that it may have been used by smugglers to hide their illegal contraband.

AN AIRMAN'S GRAVE WITH AN AEROPLANE-SHAPED GARDEN

On a hilltop just to the south of Beaminster is the 'Airman's Grave' – the unusual burial-place of Lt William Rhodes-Moorhouse, who was killed in action in 1915 – and who was the first airman ever to be awarded the VC.

He was wounded on a bombing raid over France, but just managed to get back to his base at Merville. Sadly, he died the next day, and his body was brought back to Dorset where he lived in the beautiful Tudor manor house of Parnham.

His grave is on the spot where he had intended to build a summer-house from which to enjoy the beautiful panoramic views. To commemorate his tragic death, there is a garden shaped like an aeroplane, which is still planted annually with forget-me-nots.

THE CARPENTER'S COFFIN

Thomas Hardy loved a tale with a macabre twist, and went to the trouble of verifying this one told to him by a servant when he lived at Wimborne. It was about a carpenter who was of very small stature. It happened that this carpenter was making a coffin, and unfortunately he had just discovered that he had made it too short. An onlooker standing by made a sneering joke: 'Anybody would think you'd made it for yourself, John!' The carpenter simply said 'Ah – they would!' and dropped down dead.

CRUMPLER'S COFFIN – CARVED ON AN OAK-TREE

In a field near Lytchett Matravers is a tree known as the Bull Oak, on which is carved a coffin and the inscription 'SC 1849'. This carving, made by the villagers of Lytchett, is in memory of Samuel Crumpler, a farmer who owned the field in the early nineteenth century. He was unpopular with the villagers who wanted to walk through one of his fields but couldn't because he kept a ferocious bull in it, which obviously made access difficult.

Samuel Crumpler pooh-poohed the idea that his bull was at all dangerous, and just to prove his point, he took a walk through the field himself. Naturally enough, the bull put its head down and charged. Poor Crumpler was gored to death just beside the oak tree – which instantly became known as the 'Bull Oak'. 'SC 1849' is a poignant reminder of this fatal event.

A SAINT BURIED IN HER OWN DORSET CHURCH

Few people outside Dorset know about St Wite – otherwise variously spelt as White, Whyte, Witta, or even Candida – which is simply the Latin word for 'white'. Nevertheless she is famous in the county, especially in the little Dorset village of Whitchurch Canonicorum, which is named after her – meaning 'church of St Wite belonging to the canons.' (The canons thus referred to were those of Salisbury cathedral, who once owned the manor house here.)

The true identity of St Wite is a bit of a puzzle. According to one ancient legend – and there are several – she was a Breton princess living in the fifth century, who was brought over to England by the Saxons, only to be murdered by the Vikings. Extra fanciful tales speak of her being captured by pirates, having her hand chopped off and walking back to Brittany over the sea.

Whoever she was, two facts are certain. The first is that she was believed to have the power of curing ailments. Indeed, there are three large holes in the side of her shrine here, to enable sick folk to put their hands close to her holy bones, hoping for a miraculous cure. The second is that when her tomb was opened up in 1900, the bones of a small woman aged about forty were discovered.

The shrine of the Saxon saint, St Wite. The three openings were used to enable the faithful to get nearer to the saint and her healing virtues.

St Wite's tomb has the distinction of being one of only two shrines still remaining in England and still containing their original saintly occupants – the other one being no less a personage than King Edward the Confessor, lying within his shrine in Westminster Abbey.

Visitors to Whitchurch Canonicorum may enjoy some splendid carvings, including a small panel depicting a Viking ship high on the tower wall. And even now, it's not unknown to find scraps of paper bearing hand-written prayers pushed into the holes at the side of St Wite's shrine.

NEITHER WITHIN NOR WITHOUT, AND NEITHER BELOW NOR ABOVE

In Wimborne Minster is the famous and eccentric coffin of Anthony Ettricke, an eminent seventeenth-century lawyer. He was a local boy made good, for he attended Wimborne Grammar School and went to Trinity College, Oxford. He became Recorder and Magistrate of Poole and in this position he was responsible for committing the Duke of Monmouth for trial when the Duke was captured locally after the battle of Sedgemore.

The story of the tomb is that he was so offended by the inhabitants of Wimborne that he swore he would not be buried within the

Minster nor without it, and neither below nor above the ground. Some time later when his temper had cooled down, he became sorry for this outburst, for he wanted to be buried among his ancestors. So, with all of his lawyer's cunning, he gained permission for his coffin to be placed in a recess in the Minster's wall. It is there still – a large black coffin, raised in its specially made recess, and 'neither within the church nor without it – neither below the ground nor above it'.

Oddly, he firmly believed he would die in 1693, so he had this date inscribed on his coffin. However, he lived on for another ten years, dying in 1703. The changed date is easily seen, rather clumsily done, on the side of the coffin.

A KING'S MEMORIAL – FIVE CENTURIES AFTER HIS DEATH

In the Sanctuary of Wimborne Minster is a brass memorial to the Saxon King Ethelred I (reigned 866–71). It is a small engraving of the king, wearing a crown and holding a sceptre – astonishingly not made until about AD 1440. It measures 21½ inches by 13¼ inches (55cm x 34cm). It is unique in being the only royal brass in the country.

It is strange that such a memorial should be placed here so long after the death of Ethelred, who was killed in 871, fighting the Danes. Ethelred's younger brother, Alfred, came to his funeral here in Wimborne, knowing that he was about to become king, as successor to his brother.

This king must not be confused with Ethelred 'the Unready' who reigned 978–1016 and was in fact King Ethelred II.

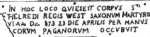

Memorial brass to King Ethelred I.
Ethelred was buried in Wimborne in 871,
having died of wounds sustained while fighting
the Danes. The inscription has the wrong date!

A COMMUNIST DISSIDENT POKED WITH A POISONED UMBRELLA

Perhaps memories are fading now, but a huge scandal erupted in 1978 when a Bulgarian writer and dissident, Georgi Markov, was poked in the leg by a poisoned umbrella as he was walking over Waterloo Bridge in London. The poison killed him, and to this day the assassin has never been found.

Surprisingly, he is buried in the Dorset village of Whitchurch Canonicorum. In February 1991 the first post-communist President of Bulgaria, Zhelyu Zhelev, paid a state visit to Britain, and made a special trip to Dorset to lay a wreath on Markov's grave. The tombstone in the churchyard of Whitchurch Canonicorum reads:

IN MEMORY OF
Georgi Ivanov Markov
Novelist and Playwright
Most dearly beloved
By his Wife Annabel
His Daughter Sasha
Born Sofia 1.3.39
Died London 11.9.78
IN THE CAUSE OF FREEDOM

A TRAGIC MASS BURIAL

A memorial stone stands against the church wall at Wyke Regis recording the tragedy in 1815 when the East Indiaman *Alexander* was wrecked in the bay – 140 crew and passengers, including women and children, were given a mass burial here.

A LIFE SPANNING THREE CENTURIES

In the churchyard at Halstock is a tombstone in memory of John Pitt, who died aged 102, and whose life extended into three centuries. He was born on 16 January 1799 and died on 20 January 1901. He lived during the reigns of four monarchs – George III, George IV, William IV and Queen Victoria. If only he had lived just two more days, he would have also been alive in the reign of Edward VII!

3

BOOKS & WRITERS

Some writers have written about Dorset, others were born in Dorset, and yet others have lived and written in Dorset. Of course, some belong to more than one group. Thomas Hardy, who falls into all three groups, is given a separate chapter elsewhere.

WRITERS ABOUT DORSET

Daniel Defoe (1661–1731)
The section on Dorset in Defoe's *Tour through England and Wales*, published in 1724, is brief and inevitably very out-of-date. Nevertheless it has its interest and charm. It is full of inaccuracies and prejudices, but who can fail to be fascinated by his remark that Wimborne Minster possessed 'a most exquisite spire, finer and taller, if fame lyes not, than that at Salisbury'? Defoe had personally taken part in the Monmouth Rebellion in 1685, so when writing of Monmouth's landing at Lyme Regis, he tactfully remarks 'I need say nothing, the history of it being so recent in the memory of so many living.'

Sir Frederick Treves (1853–1923)
Frederick Treves was born in Dorchester, and although he was thirteen years younger than Thomas Hardy, the two men became close friends in later life. Treves was one of William Barnes's pupils.

Treves became a professor at the Royal College of Surgeons and was a founder of the Red Cross Society. He is famous, too, for having saved the life of King Edward VII by performing an operation for appendicitis on the king just two days before he was due to be crowned in 1902. At that time, this operation was extremely dangerous, and right up to the last moment the king flatly refused to be operated upon. Only when he was told that it was a matter of an operation or death did King Edward consent. Luckily, Treves succeeded triumphantly, and was rewarded by being made a baronet.

As an author, Treves is remembered for his book *Highways and Byways of Dorset*. For this, in 1904–5, in his early fifties, Treves cycled more than 2,000 miles throughout the county to gather material for his book, which was published in 1906 – much of it being still relevant today.

Hermann Lea (1869–unknown)

Hermann Lea's *Thomas Hardy's Wessex*, first published in 1913, is essential for anyone seriously interested in the background of Hardy's writings. Importantly, Lea was a close personal friend of Hardy, who collaborated with him in producing this work. Hardy himself proof-read it to ensure there were no inaccuracies. Hermann Lea has been described as a builder, beekeeper, gardener, poultry-keeper, cyclist, water-diviner, animal-lover, inventor, photographer, author and 'automobilist'.

He was something of an eccentric, who came to live in Puddletown to learn farming and became interested in Hardy's Wessex first as a hobby and then as a consuming passion. Although he was almost thirty years younger than Hardy, the two men found much in common, and with his interest in photography, Lea produced a remarkable set of illustrations featuring all the places mentioned in each of Hardy's works. Hardy enjoyed cycling with Lea to show him places he had described, and in his later years Hardy was driven around Dorset in the motor-cars which were in Lea's proud possession.

In his introduction to *Thomas Hardy's Wessex*, Hermann Lea made the bold claim that he had 'travelled over practically all the main roads, and many of the lanes and by-roads, traversing more than 150,000 miles on a cycle, in a car [and] on foot.'

Arthur Mee (1875–1943)

Arthur Mee was an incredibly prolific writer and editor, and it can hardly be believed that he wrote all the works published under his name. Nevertheless, although it is somewhat dated, Mee's *Dorset* in *The King's England* series, provides a useful inventory of what can – or could – be seen in all its towns and villages.

Interestingly, Mee's book on Dorset contains items which can no longer be seen, for it was first published in June 1939, less than three months before the outbreak of the Second World War.

Poignantly he gives a description of Tyneham, the village soon to be abandoned and left to the army and ruin (see page 147). Here are some extracts from his description:

> TYNEHAM. It lies in beautiful country, a hamlet on the splendid coast a few miles from Corfe Castle. In a cluster of trees hides an Elizabethan mansion, but Tyneham is older than Elizabeth, for it was part of Roman England, and here have been found those curious fragments of the past known as Kimmeridge Coal Money. In a grave that was opened a Roman urn was found filled with these small things, black and shaped like coins, and for a long time they were mysterious. It has now been settled that they are the centres falling out from rings cut by the Romans from Kimmeridge shale.
>
> The little church has a medallion of old glass, and a most beautiful window of our own time made by Martin Travers, showing the Mother and Child under a growing tree against a clear light-giving background. The window is in three scenes, and on either side is a picture of Tyneham life, one showing men at the plough, the other men drawing in a boat.

Jo Draper

Without doubt, one of the best books on Dorset is Jo Draper's *Dorset – the Complete Guide*, first published in 1986 and subsequently revised and reprinted. This '*Complete Guide*' is exactly what it says, and contains a succinct account of virtually every aspect of the county. As editor for the Dorset Natural History and Archaeological Society, Jo Draper took three years to complete this superbly illustrated guide, and she was proud to claim that she visited every entry mentioned in the text.

Rodney Legg

No one, surely, has ever been more passionate about any county as Rodney Legg is about Dorset. He has written literally countless articles and many books (125 at the last count) about almost every conceivable aspect of the county. He has personally tramped thousands of miles in search of the material for his books, which are always meticulously researched and lucidly written. Bookshops and websites are testimony to his work. Sadly, Rodney died on July 2011, aged only 63.

WRITERS BORN IN DORSET

William Barnes (1801–86), born in Bagber
Everyone who knows Dorset must know of this learned old
parson/schoolmaster. His statue stands outside St Peter's Church
in High West Street in Dorchester. He is dressed in clerical garb
just as he would have appeared as he walked to his little school
just a hundred yards away, in South Street.

Barnes's gentle poems in the Dorset dialect are some of the most
idyllic in the language, and thanks to Vaughan Williams's music,
his 'Linden Lea' is widely known and loved. However, few people
listening to this are fully aware of just what an extraordinary
genius William Barnes was – although his life was humdrum and
uneventful.

He was, in his own words, 'born at Rush-hay, farmling at Bagber
in the Parish of Sturminster Newton in the Vale of Blackmore' –
the heart of rural Dorset. He left school at thirteen and started
work as a solicitor's clerk. However, he read voraciously,
constantly educating himself in a huge variety of subjects. Aged
about twenty-three he started up a school in Mere, just over the
county border in Wiltshire, and then aged thirty-five he came
back to 'the home of my heart' to start his school in South Street,
Dorchester. He never left Dorset again except on occasional trips.

Largely educating himself over the years, he was ordained at
forty-six, gained his Cambridge BD degree aged fifty, and poured
out scores of articles on a huge variety of subjects, writing many
scholarly books on philology, quoting from over 70 different
languages. He was fluent in Greek and Latin, many modern
European languages and was familiar with Welsh, Persian and
Urdu. He wrote more than 800 poems and, notably, he was a
passionate advocate of restoring Anglo-Saxon as the principal
source of English vocabulary. He lectured locally, and was the
principal force in the establishment of Dorchester's museum.

He married his teenage sweetheart, Julia Miles, daughter of an
excise officer in Dorchester, and they had six children. The tragedy
of his life was Julia's early death, and for the rest of his life he
ended his daily diary (which he wrote in Italian!) with a plaintive
single word, the Italian version of her name, *Giulia*.

Despite his huge gifts and immense literary output, Barnes was 'morbidly modest' and never sought fame or fortune. First a schoolmaster, he became a country parson for the last twenty-four years of his life. Perhaps his most enduring legacy was that he was the friend and mentor of the young Thomas Hardy, who was inspired in many ways by this shy and eccentric genius.

LINDEN LEA and the Welsh cynghanedd

Many who know and love William Barnes's poem *My Orcha'd in Linden Lea* are completely unaware of the sophisticated artistry which goes into its composition. For most readers, it is a triumph of simplicity – but it is a simplicity which conceals an elaborate art form.

Barnes the philologist had studied Celtic literature, and knew of the Welsh poetic device known as the *cynghanedd,* in which there is a repetition of consonantal sounds in the two parts of a line divided by a caesura or small break.

In *Linden Lea* the consonants are d n l – sounds which liltingly appear in the refrain:

> 'Do lean down low in linden lea'

Other examples in Barnes's poetry: 'In our abode in Arby Wood' and 'An' love to roost, where they can live at rest'.

The verbal magic is there – but unless it's pointed out, it is appreciated only subconsciously.

Thomas Bell (1792–1880), born in Poole

Son of a surgeon, Bell became a dentist, but his passion was the study of British wildlife. He produced three standards works: *History of British Quadrupeds* (1837), *History of British Reptiles* (1839), and *History of British Stalk-eyed Crustacea* (1853). He retired to Selborne and edited Gilbert White's *Natural History of Selborne.*

John Gould (1804–81), born in Lyme Regis

Perhaps only specialist ornithologists can properly appreciate the extraordinary books of bird illustrations that John Gould produced. He has been called 'the supreme ornithologist of all time,' for he discovered, described, and illustrated more species of birds than anyone else has ever done – or can ever do, for he has pre-empted any would-be follower. There are simply no more birds to discover!

He became curator and preserver (taxidermist) to the Zoological Society in London, travelling widely to collect specimens and engaging others to provide skins for the museum. His superb collections of illustrations are to be found in *Birds of Europe* (five vols 1832–7), *Birds of Australia* (seven vols 1840–8), *Birds of Asia* (1849–83) and *Birds of England* (1862–73).

His books are among the rarest in the world – in 1987 a set of his works fetched £400,000.

In all, he produced 2,999 illustrations (surely he could have done just one more), and to produce these at the rate of two a week would have taken Gould more than twenty-eight years without a break!

Marguerite Radclyffe Hall (1886–1943), born in Durley Road, Bournemouth (on the site now occupied by the Durley Grange Hotel)
Radclyffe Hall is seldom remembered now, but in the 1920s she won acclaim for several collections of poetry and also for her novels, *The Forge* (1924), *The Unlit Lamp* (1924) and *Adam's Breed* (1926), which won the Femina Vie Heureuse and Tait-Black Memorial prizes.

Then in 1928 all hell broke loose when she produced her next novel, *The Well of Loneliness*. Shock and horror – it was a novel about lesbianism! It was far too much for the Home Secretary, who declared it to be 'inherently obscene,' and banned it forthwith. It was, however, published in Paris, and secretly shipped back to Britain, and it was also sold in the United States. Undeterred, Radclyffe Hall continued writing more novels until her death. She is buried in Highgate Cemetery in London.

One newspaper editor, reviewing this lesbian-based novel, said that he would rather 'give a healthy child prussic acid to drink than read such an obnoxious book.' The fact is, the obscenity is so slight that today it is hardly noticed. Arguably the most explicit line was 'And that night they were not divided.' No wonder Virginia Woolf complained, 'The dullness of the book is such that . . . one simply can't keep one's eyes on the page.'

Ralph Wightman (1901–71)

Quintessentially a Dorset man, born in Piddletrenthide, son of a farmer, broadcaster, and author of thirteen books, written between 1948 and 1970, all of which had farming and the countryside, Dorset and Wessex as their themes. *Abiding Things* (1962) and *Portrait of Dorset* (1965) are two of his works which are still well worth reading. His gentle Dorset voice and broad accents were instantly recognisable on popular radio discussion programmes and he will be long remembered.

Robert Young (1810–1908)

A remarkable old character who was a tailor lived and worked most of his life in his native town of Sturminster Newton. He had worked for a while in London and Poole, so his horizons had been broadened a little. However, his claim to literary fame rests on poems he wrote in the Dorset dialect.

He was a friend of William Barnes, and owned Riverside, the house at Sturminster Newton which he rented out for two years to Thomas and Emma Hardy shortly after their marriage.

Robert Young described himself as 'An Olde Dorset Songster' and wrote some comic poems under the name of Rabin Hill. Especially popular was his verse tale: 'Rabin Hill's Visit to the Railway: What he Zeed and Done and What he Zed About It'. His brief autobiography, *Early Years – Recollections of Life in Sturminster Newton in the early nineteenth century* is a fascinating document of social history.

THE POWYS BROTHERS . . .

. . . are so closely linked with Dorset that it comes as a surprise to realise that only one of them – Llewellyn Powys – was actually born in Dorset. Nevertheless, they may be regarded, perhaps, as honorary Dorset products. They were members of a family of eleven – children of the Revd Charles Francis Powys and his wife Mary – claiming descent from Welsh princes and also through their mother from John Donne and William Cowper. Between them, these four Powys brothers wrote more than forty books – novels, short stories, and autobiographies – some of which have been 'the subject of much debate' and 'defy classification'.

John Cowper Powys (1872–1964), born at Shirley in Derbyshire
Educated at Sherborne School, his novels include *A Glastonbury Romance* (1932), *Weymouth Sands* (1934) and *Maiden Castle* (1936). After death, his ashes were cast into the sea from Chesil Beach at Abbotsbury.

Littleton C. Powys (1874–1955)
Taught at Sherborne School and wrote his autobiography, *The Joy of It* (1937). He also edited the letters of Elizabeth Myers.

Llewellyn Powys (1884–1939), born in Dorchester
Educated at Sherborne School, after a life in Kenya and New York he returned to live and die in Chaldon Herring. He is remembered for his collections of essays: *Thirteen Worthies, Somerset and Dorset Essays, A Baker's Dozen,* and others.

Theodore Francis Powys ('T.F.') (1875–1955)
He lived at East Chaldon and later at Mappowder, where he lived in solitude, 'searching for God' and going to church alone on weekdays but never to a service on Sundays.

T.F. Powys was arguably the most interesting and most startlingly original writer of them all, with his *Fables* and *Mr Weston's Good Wine*. It's recorded that Thomas Hardy literally jumped out of his chair with surprise and delight when he first came across T.F. Powys's works. In some ways, T.F. Powys could be regarded as a natural literary descendant of Hardy himself.

WRITERS WHO HAVE LIVED AND WRITTEN IN DORSET

Enid Blyton (1897–1968)
For twenty years Blyton regularly spent her holidays in Swanage. Statistics concerning Enid Blyton's output of children's books are almost unbelievable, with her 753 titles produced over 45 years –

averaging 16 books a year. She habitually wrote 10,000 words a day, and easily completed a book in a week. More than 600 million copies of her books have been sold, and they have been translated into about 90 languages. Even in the twenty-first century sales of her books continue to amaze – amounting to millions of copies annually.

Her second husband bought a farm in Dorset and together they bought the Isle of Purbeck Golf Club. Many of the locations in her books were inspired by her love of this part of Dorset, including:

Kirrin Castle	Corfe Castle
Whispering Island	Brownsea Island
Mystery Moor	heath between Stoborough and Corfe
Finniston Farm	her own farm at Sturminster Newton

. . . And PC Plod is thought to have been based on a genial local bobby – the late PC Christopher Rone of Studland.

Enid and her husband would take delight in swimming round the piers in Swanage before their evening dinner. Somewhat eccentric, she is said to have enjoyed playing tennis in the nude. Sadly, she died suffering from Alzheimer's disease, aged only seventy-one.

Rupert Brooke (1887–1915)
Rupert Brooke was stationed only briefly at Bovington Camp during the First World War, but while he was there he wrote one of the most famous of all English war poems – the sonnet beginning:

> If I should die, think only this of me:
> That there's some corner of a foreign field
> That is for ever England.

In fact, the 'foreign field' was to be the Greek island of Skyros, where he was buried in April 1915 after dying of blood poisoning.

Cumberland Clark (1862–1941)
Celebrating the charms of Bournemouth in memorably bad verse, Cumberland Clark has achieved cult status as arguably Britain's most excruciatingly awful poet, far outstripping Scotland's William McGonagall's bid for the title. His interests, however, ranged widely and among his output of 72 books there were some serious prose works.

His collection of verse, *The Bournemouth Song Book*, has to be read to be believed. Jewel after jewel might be quoted, but here are a few to whet appetites:

The New Pavilion

The splendid new Pavilion
Can cater for the million
This ambitious undertaking
Needed courage in the making,
A long, long time it took to build, although no time was lost,
A quarter of a million pounds was said to be the cost

Beale's
(a privately-owned department store in Bournemouth)

When people go to shop at Beale's
How happy everybody feels!
They find no gloom in any room
For all is gay and gladsome.
Around the store bright smiles you see,
It's great! You take the tip from me;
I've been there and I've had some.

Patriotically, during the Second World War, he used his poetic skills to produce *War Songs of the Allies* containing the chirpily brave verse:

Let the bombs bounce round above us,
And the shells come whizzing by,
Down in our Air-Raid Shelter
We'll be cosy, you and I.

With ironic precision, a German plane flew over Bournemouth on 10 April 1941, dropped its bomb and killed him.

John Fowles (1926–2005)
Fowles lived for almost 40 years at Belmont House in Lyme Regis. In 2008 *The Times* listed John Fowles among its list of 'The 50 greatest British writers'. A novelist of great distinction, he is probably mostly remembered for *The French Lieutenant's Woman*, published in 1969 and made into a film in 1981 with

the screenplay by Harold Pinter. Belmont House – also associated with Eleanor Coade, the inventor of Coade Stone – was used as a setting for parts of this film.

Apart from *The Collector* (1963) and *The Magus* (1965), John Fowles wrote all his novels and non-fiction works at Lyme Regis, where he served for a while as curator of the local museum.

John Keats (1795–1821)

Keats wrote his last poem on the Dorset coast on 30 September 1820. It was just a few hours spent ashore – most probably at Lulworth Cove – that gave Keats a moment of peaceful reflection to write this last poem. He was leaving England for ever, travelling by boat to Rome, and the ship was temporarily at anchor, waiting for a favourable wind. Within months Keats was to die of tuberculosis in Italy, and his own medical training told him that he was terminally ill. Also, in hopeless grief, he was in love.

In these circumstances, the poem he wrote is one of the most poignant he composed, written on a blank page in his book of Shakespeare's verse:

'Bright star! would I were steadfast as thou art –'

Exactly one hundred years later, in September 1920, another poet, Thomas Hardy, with his usual fine appreciation of life's significant moments, captured the scene in his own poem 'At Lulworth Cove a Century Back' –

' – That man goes to Rome – to death, despair;
And no one notes him now but you and I:
A hundred years, and the world will follow him there,
And bend with reverence where his ashes lie.'

William Kethe (d. 1608)

William Kethe's (rector of Child Okeford, 1561–94) claim to fame rests on his book of metrical psalms, the best-known of which is 'All People that on Earth Do Dwell' – a version of Psalm 100. This 'simple but majestic paraphrase' has the distinction of being the earliest hymn written in the English language which is still in general use today.

William Kethe left Britain during the reign of the catholic Queen Mary Tudor, and spent time in Geneva helping to translate the Bible into English as well as compiling and writing his metrical psalms. He returned to England when the Protestant Elizabeth I became queen, and he became chaplain to the forces under the Earl of Warwick in 1563. In later life he opted to be the rector in the quiet village of Child Okeford.

Child Okeford has a link to another famous hymn – for it was in 1871 in the church of St Nicholas there that the first public performance of the music for 'Onward Christian Soldiers' was heard. Arthur Sullivan had not yet formed his association with W.S. Gilbert, but he was already gaining success and fame for his compositions. He was staying at Hanford House, near Child Okeford, when he wrote this hymn tune specially to fit the words, and the title he gave the tune – 'St Gertrude' refers not to a saint, but to his hostess at Hanford House, whose name was Gertrude. Hanford House is now an independent girls' school.

Beverley Naidoo (1943–)

Beverley Naidoo (who now lives in Bournemouth) was born in South Africa and was imprisoned in solitary confinement in 1964 for her opposition to Apartheid. Subsequently she has studied at York University and has written many books about South Africa and its troubles. Her first novel for children, *Journey to Jo'burg,* 1985, was banned in South Africa until 1991.

Her many awards include The Arts Council's Writers' Award in 1999, The Carnegie Medal in 2000, and The Los Angeles Times Book Prize (Young Adult Fiction) in 2001.

Robert Louis Stevenson (1850–94)

Stevenson, in his mid-thirties, lived in Bournemouth from 1884 to 1887 with his newly-wed American wife and step-son and wrote *Kidnapped* and *The Strange Case of Dr Jeykll and Mr Hyde* while in the town. Unfortunately the house, which they named 'Skerryvore', was so badly damaged by a landmine in the Second World War that it had to be demolished.

The site is now a garden of rest, with the footings of the house laid out in stone, and a 4ft-tall stone lighthouse placed there – a large model of the Skerryvore lighthouse designed by his uncle, Alan Stevenson.

Despite the fact that he intensely disliked *Tess of the D'Urbervilles*, Stevenson wrote to Thomas Hardy to ask permission to visit him at Max Gate. Afterwards, Stevenson's wife Fanny noted that Hardy was 'a quite pathetic figure', 'a pale, gentle, frightened little man, that one felt an instinctive tenderness for, with a wife – ugly is no word for it.'

The bridge at Alum Chine in Bournemouth has a plaque commemorating Stevenson's stay in Bournemouth where he 'lived like a weevil in a biscuit' – his own words!

Flora Thompson (1876–1947)
Flora Thompson, whose books inspired the TV series *Lark Rise to Candleford,* and its charismatic postmistress, was a postmistress's assistant herself. She married a post office clerk and they settled in Winton, a suburb of Bournemouth, where her husband worked in Bournemouth's main post office. It was thanks to Winton Public Library, which opened just as the Thompsons came to live there, that Flora gained her love of books and her passionate desire to write.

It was in 1911, during her time in Winton, that Flora had the good fortune to win an essay competition in *The Ladies' Companion* for a 300-word piece on Jane Austen. From then on her enthusiasm knew no bounds, and she embarked on a lifetime of writing short stories and magazine and newspaper articles.

Her three books, *Lark Rise* (1939), *Over to Candleford* (1941), and *Candleford Green* (1943) were published as a trilogy – *Lark Rise to Candleford* – in 1945.

William Wordsworth (1770–1850)
Wordsworth is so inseparably linked with the Lake District that it comes as something of a surprise to realise that he spent two of the most important years of his life in a secluded spot in Dorset. He and his sister Dorothy had the good fortune to be offered the use of Racedown Lodge absolutely rent-free between 1795 and 1797. Racedown is a square-built house near the village of Birdsmoor

Gate, about half-way between Lyme Regis and Crewkerne, and it is about 6 miles from the coast.

Staying in Dorset was a turning-point in Wordsworth's life, for he needed some time for peace and quiet after his turbulent time in France. The months he spent here enabled him to restore his creative powers, and, most importantly of all, it was at Racedown in June 1797 that he and Dorothy met his inspirational friend and collaborator, Samuel Taylor Coleridge, who was then living at Nether Stowey in Somerset. 'We both have a distinctive remembrance of his arrival,' Wordsworth wrote more than forty years later. 'He did not keep to the high road but leaped over a gate and bounded down a pathless field by which he cut off an angle.'

It was to be just one year later, in 1798, that the two poets were to change the course of English poetry for ever with the publication of their *Lyrical Ballads.*

4

ABBEYS & CHURCHES

The Christian past permeates Dorset. Churches, abbeys, place-names, folklore and legends – everything points to centuries of profound Christian faith. Many of the sacred buildings go back to a time almost unimaginable today. Here are some reminders of Dorset's centuries of faith.

In a recent book, *England's Thousand Best Churches*, Simon Jenkins judged his buildings by awarding up to five stars for the most outstanding. In Dorset, he gave Sherborne Abbey and Christchurch Priory the prestigious five-star rating.

Similarly, he awarded four stars to Bournemouth St Peter, Bournemouth St Stephen, Milton Abbey and Wimborne Minster.

Three stars went to Poole St Osmund and Puddletown; two stars to Bere Regis, Blandford Forum, Charlton Marshall, Kingston (Isle of Purbeck), Moreton, Studland, Trent, Whitchurch Canonicorum and Winterborne Tomson; and one star went to Affpuddle, Beaminster, Cattistock, Cerne Abbas, Chalbury, Charminster, Iwerne Minster, Lyme Regis, Portland St George, Tarrant Crawford, and both St Aldhelm and St Nicholas in Worth Matravers.

So, starting with the two 'five-star' buildings. . . .

SHERBORNE ABBEY, DORSET'S EX-CATHEDRAL

There has been no cathedral in Dorset since the time of William the Conqueror. Previously, however, for 370 years Dorset had possessed a Saxon cathedral in Sherborne with a succession of no fewer than 27 bishops – from 705, when St Aldhelm became its first bishop, to 1075, when the see was moved to Old Sarum, whereupon the 27th Bishop of Sherborne became the 1st Bishop of Salisbury. Sherborne had been too far west for William the Conqueror's liking, so he shifted the see nearer to Winchester and London. By this means, the ever-vigilant Conqueror could keep his eye on things. From then on until the time of Henry VIII Sherborne Abbey continued to be simply the home of monks.

At the Dissolution of the Monasteries in 1539, the people of Sherborne were able to buy the abbey for use as their parish church. They paid 100 marks (£66 13s 4d – 13s and 4d was one-third of a pound which equals about 66p in decimal currency) for it.

The monks' dwelling-areas of Sherborne Abbey were turned into a school, thanks to the boy king, Edward VI. In 1550 he re-founded the old monastic school as King Edward's School – a free grammar school for local boys. His portrait hangs there still.

A riot, a fire, a punishment, and beautifully restored, Sherborne Abbey has a complicated history – but broadly speaking most of what we see today is the result of a huge makeover after a great fire in 1437. In that year the local citizens staged a great revolt against the abbot and his monks, principally over their right to have their own font in a part of the abbey (now lost) which they were using for parish services.

In the course of this revolt one of the parish priests of the town actually shot a flaming arrow into the monks' part of the abbey – and the results were catastrophic. John Leland, the 'King's Antiquarie' to Henry VIII, relates what happened:

> . . . after the variance growing to a plain sedition, by the men of an Earl of Huntingdon, laying in those quarters and taking the townsmen's part, and the Bishop of Salisbury the monks' part, a priest . . . shot a shaft with fire into the top of that part of (the abbey) that divided the east part that the monks used from that which the townsmen used; and the partition, chancing at that time to be thatched in the roof, was set afire, and consequently the whole church, the lead and bells melted, was defaced.

After this, the abbot forced the rebellious townsfolk to pay for the reconstruction of the abbey – and to pay for the very best that could be produced. The gorgeous interior, with its magically beautiful fan-vaulted roof, is the result!

The beauty of Sherborne Abbey is enhanced by the builders' choice of local Ham Hill stone from a quarry only 13 miles away, at Hamdon Hill – 'a glorious material warmer than even the most creamy Cotswold,' as one writer described it, and as Alec Clifton-Taylor wrote, 'in the contemplation of these rich, golden brown surfaces . . . the eye may find insatiable pleasure.'

There is much to enjoy in Sherborne Abbey, but in particular the carved detail in the roof bosses should not be missed (heraldic shields, Tudor roses, a mermaid combing her hair, a dog chewing a bone, an owl mobbed by birds, Green Men, and the initials H.E., commemorating the marriage of Henry VII with Elizabeth of York . . . and many more).

Equally not to be missed are ten misericords under the seats in the choir. Scenes here include a woman beating her husband and a schoolmaster beating a boy on his bottom. (Notice the weals on the boy's bottom – and the monkey faces of the boy's fellow pupils who are looking on, evidently enjoying the sight!)

CHRISTCHURCH PRIORY, A CHURCH BUILT BY CHRIST HIMSELF

The very name 'Christchurch' tells the legendary story of how Christ himself came to help with the carpentry work when it was being built. Originally, the town of Christchurch was called 'Twynham', signifying that it was a town on two rivers, situated where the rivers Avon and Stour join. It was an important and thriving port in the early Middle Ages, so it was a natural site for the Normans to build a new and imposing church to replace a little Saxon church which had been there since the seventh century.

The crucial story about the origin of Christchurch is that the Norman builders first decided to raise a building on St Catherine's Hill – about a mile and a half away. However, every night as the work began, various materials disappeared from the site, and turned up at the original holy site of the old church. Obviously God was making a point about where He wanted the new church to be built!

Thus divinely guided, the builders went back to the site indicated. But then, as work continued, an extra carpenter appeared among them, who never came for meals or for pay. One day, a huge wooden beam was cut too short for the place it was to occupy. It was a major disaster. However, the following day, to everyone's amazement, not only was the heavy beam found to be restored to the correct length, but it had miraculously been put in place. Even more mysterious was the fact that the anonymous carpenter had disappeared. Obviously, he must have been the 'Carpenter of Nazareth' himself. The story of the 'Miraculous Beam' became famous – so much so that the church became known as 'Christ's Church', and the town itself changed its name from Twynham to Christchurch.

The importance of the priory being literally 'Christ's church' led to its becoming a major attraction for pilgrims. Hundreds came from far and wide, so that the town and the priory gained wealth and prestige. The 'Miraculous Beam' is still there, for all to see.

Christchurch Priory is the largest parish church in Britain, with an approximate floor area of 18,300 sq ft.

Its total length is 311ft (94.8m) – the longest of any parish church in England.

The north porch is probably the largest of its kind in England, 40ft long (12.2m) with walls 6ft (1.82m) thick. It was a useful meeting-place, and it was where the prior met the townsfolk, to discuss their problems.

Two of its bells are reckoned to be the oldest in the country still to be rung regularly.

Above the Lady Chapel is St Michael's Loft Museum – containing much of interest concerning the history of the priory. Until 1869 this room was the home of Christchurch Grammar School.

There are many lovely and interesting things to see in Christchurch Priory. Not to be missed are the fascinating wooden carvings on the misericords and bench ends (see the fox dressed as a friar, preaching to geese), or the stone carvings on the capitals (including a two-headed Judas!), or the wonderful ceiling in the Salisbury chantry, or the poignant statue of Mary Shelley (authoress of

Frankenstein) grieving over the dead body of her drowned husband, the Romantic poet, Percy Bysshe Shelley.

The Salisbury Chantry, in the north quire aisle, was built in 1529 by Margaret, Countess of Salisbury, née Plantagenet, as a tomb for herself and her son, Cardinal Pole. She was the niece of Edward IV and Richard III, and as such was the last living member of the Plantagenet dynasty. When Henry VIII proclaimed himself Head of the Church in England, Cardinal Pole, living in Rome at the time, bitterly criticised the king. Henry was so angry that in revenge he imprisoned the ageing Countess of Salisbury and ruthlessly ordered her execution. The proud old countess refused to lay her head down on the block at the Tower of London. As she struggled to her feet, she was literally hacked to pieces as she stood. She is buried in the chapel of St Peter ad Vincula in the Tower. For that reason, the Salisbury Chantry in Christchurch Priory contains no body. Nevertheless, pilgrims have visited this exquisite chantry for centuries, offering prayers in her memory. The Countess of Salisbury was beatified in 1886 and is now venerated as a Catholic martyr.

Christchurch Priory was founded in 1094 by Ranulf Flambard, a colourful character who rose to become the most powerful man in the country under the unpopular King William II (son of the conqueror, and nicknamed 'Rufus' because of his flaming red hair). Flambard was notoriously grasping, and unscrupulously amassed great wealth. When Rufus died, his successor Henry I immediately flung Flambard into the Tower of London for embezzlement – he was the Tower's first prisoner. Flambard managed to escape – traditionally by having a barrel of wine sent in to him, with a rope hidden inside. He made his captors drunk and then used the rope to clamber out of his prison window.

In the gardens to the south of Christchurch Priory is a jolly piece of modern sculpture by Jonathan Sells, showing Ranulf Flambard making his escape. Flambard's life was quite extraordinary – and he later became Bishop of Durham, where he had a hand in building the cathedral.

For all its beauty, interest and history, Christchurch Priory has been described thus, 'of all the great churches of England, Christchurch is probably the least well known.'

WIMBORNE MINSTER, THE 'SPOTTED DOG' CHURCH

The exterior of Wimborne Minster has been called 'eccentric' with its two towers, not quite a match – one being Norman and the other Perpendicular. And it has been called 'odd' and even 'unhappy' because of the unusual stonework. It has a strange spotty appearance, being constructed with a haphazard mixture of Dorset limestone and a 'very inedible-looking dark brown' pudding-stone. Alec Clifton-Taylor called this a 'spotted dog effect which is not at all happy'.

Nevertheless, despite these somewhat snooty criticisms, Wimborne Minster is much loved, always filled with visitors, and has a vibrant parish life. Its odd appearance gives it a unique attractiveness and there are very many fascinating things to see both inside and outside.

The minster is dedicated to St Cuthburga, sister to King Ine, who was king of the West Saxons from 688 to 726 – and it is the only church dedicated to her. Cuthburga founded a Benedictine Nunnery on this site in about 713.

Wimborne Minster – the 'spotted dog' church.

At one time no fewer than 500 women were being trained at St Cuthburga's nunnery – and St Boniface (*c.* 680–*c.* 754) recruited missionaries from Wimborne to help in his great task of converting the pagan tribes of Germany.

On the outside, high up on the West Tower, there is a 'Quarter Jack' – an amusing little figure of a smartly-dressed soldier in early nineteenth-century uniform. He strikes two bells every quarter of an hour. The mechanism was first made in 1612, originally with a figure of a monk to strike the bells. However, the monk was changed to the present grenadier during the Napoleonic Wars.

Inside the minster there is an extraordinarily complicated astronomical clock, which not only tells the time with a 24-hour dial, but also marks the phases of the moon. It was made before the time of Copernicus (1473–1543), who discovered that the earth moved round the sun, so the dial is made on the Ptolemaic system, showing the Earth as a black ball in the centre, with the sun and moon revolving round it. In the nineteenth century this

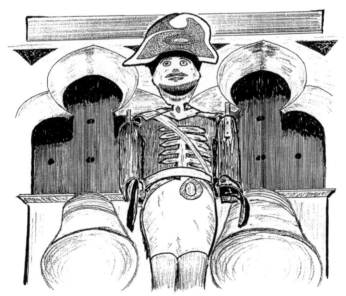

The Quarter Jack on Wimborne Minster. A brightly coloured grenadier from Napoleonic times.

clock was connected to a set of chimes which played eight tunes on ten bells. However, these jollifications were stopped after the music was sometimes deemed to be rather tactless. On one occasion the chimes gave a hearty rendering of 'Rule Britannia' just as a funeral was entering the church!

Not content with having a quarter-jack striking his bells every 15 minutes and an astronomical clock giving additional time-information, Wimborne Minster also possesses a very unusual sundial on a large four-sided pillar by the West Tower.

It is unusual because it has no fewer than *three* 'gnomons' (the metal shadow-casting elements). These enable shadows to be cast throughout a full 12-hour period, for as the sun moves around the pillar the shadows are taken up successively by each of the three gnomons on three sides of the pillar.

The older of the minster's two towers – the one in the middle, which is Norman – used to have a tall spire, until one day in 1600, with dramatic suddenness, it collapsed and fell. Here is a near-contemporary account:

> . . . I will not overpasse a strange Accident, which in our Dayes happened unto it, viz. Anno Domini 1600 (the Choire being then full of People at tenne of Clock Service, allsoe the Streets by reason of the Markett) a sudden Mist ariseing, all the Spire Steeple, being of a verie great Height, was strangely cast downe; the stones battered all the Lead, and brake much of the Timber of the Roofe of the Church, yet without anie Hurte to the People. . .

When Wimborne lost its spire, only three spires were left in the entire county: St Mary's at Iwerne Minster, St Andrew's at Trent and St Michael's at Winterborne Steepleton. Dorset is a county of towers rather than steeples. However, in the 1970s, when Bournemouth was incorporated into the county, Dorset suddenly acquired quite a number of additional nineteenth- and twentieth-century spires.

Great treasures are to be seen in a room over the thirteenth-century vestry in Wimborne Minster, for it houses a remarkable chained library. There are about 380 volumes, of which over 150 are chained. In the Middle Ages books in almost all libraries were chained because they were so rare and valuable – a single volume perhaps equalling the price of a farm.

Most of these chained books are in Latin, Greek, or Hebrew, and almost all are rare works of theology, written by scholars of the early Christian church. The oldest book is the *Regimen Animarum,* or 'Guiding of Souls' and it is dated at 1343. This is a list of the spiritual dangers which may tempt us, and the methods by which we may avoid them.

One of the books in the chained library is a rare copy of the so-called 'Breeches Bible', in which the translation of *Genesis 3:7* tells how Adam and Eve made 'breeches' for themselves out of fig-leaves, when they realised for the first time that they were naked.

'They sowed figge-leaves together and made themselves breeches'

ST PETER'S, BOURNEMOUTH, 'ONE OF THE RICHEST GOTHIC REVIVAL INTERIORS IN ENGLAND'

Situated in the very middle of the town, St Peter's is Bournemouth's 'mother church'. An earlier church was begun on this site in 1840, and a part of this was incorporated within the present building, begun just a few years later, in 1854. Over the next twenty-five years St Peter's grew simultaneously with the brand-new seaside resort, adding more and more exotic decoration to its interior. It became, and remains, one of the most ornate examples of High Victorianism to be found anywhere in England.

Its decoration is perhaps an acquired taste – but thanks to John Betjeman and the passing of the years, it can now be better appreciated. Certainly it represents the very best in Victorian ecclesiastical art. It has links with some of the greatest names in the Victorian world, and has contributions from the most celebrated artists of that century.

The architect was G.E. Street, famous also for designing the Law Courts in London.

A window here was designed and made by William Morris and Sir Edward Burne-Jones.

Much of the carving was done by Thomas Earp – including the remarkable pulpit, exhibited at the Great Exhibition in London.

Earp was Street's favourite sculptor. Possibly his finest carving here is above a doorway in a rather obscure corner, showing St Peter receiving the keys of Heaven from Jesus.

St Peter's has to be seen. It cannot be adequately described. Everywhere there is a wealth of superb carving, especially in the capitals and arches in the chancel. Particularly noteworthy is the variety of colour in the alabaster. Every inch seems to vibrate with ornate shape and sumptuous tones.

Interestingly, the chancel and sanctuary floor is made from a combination of Hopton Wood stone and Fosterly Marble, in which, on close inspection, the white flecks reveal themselves to be fossilised fish.

The choir stalls were designed by the distinguished Victorian architect, George Bodley, known to Oxford men for the tower of 'Tom Quad' at Christ Church, and to Cambridge men for the 'Bodley' buildings at King's College. In one of these stalls is a plaque commemorating the fact that William Gladstone made his last communion there in 1898.

When one learns that John Keble himself – foremost in initiating the High Church Oxford Movement – regularly worshipped here in his retirement, the whole church seems magnificently appropriate to his times.

St Peter's churchyard contains tombs and memorial stones to Lewis Tregonwell, the 'Founder of Bournemouth' in 1810; the Wollstonecrafts and Shelleys (see Bones & Burials chapter); Sir Dan Godfrey, first conductor of the Bournemouth Municipal Orchestra (now the Bournemouth Symphony Orchestra); and Constantin Silvestri, one of the twentieth century's leading conductors.

SURPRISING CATHOLIC CHURCHES IN DORSET

Catholic worship was illegal in Britain for more than 230 years – from 1558, in the reign of Queen Elizabeth I until 1791, in the reign of King George III, when the Catholic Relief Act made it possible for Catholics to worship openly once again.

The new act of parliament suddenly made it possible for new Catholic churches to be built, and Dorset has some surprisingly beautiful examples – but you have to look for them. Among the most brilliantly designed and decorated of these are:

Wardour Castle Chapel, near Shaftesbury (1770–6, extended 1789–90)
Built by the very rich Arundell family, who had always stayed resolutely Catholic, this was built before the Catholic Relief Act made it legal, so it was prudently hidden inside the wing of a new classical house which was being built.

St Mary's Chapel, Lulworth Castle (1786–7)
This was the first free-standing Roman Catholic chapel to be built in England since the Reformation. It was built by the Bastard brothers of Blandford for Thomas Weld, of Lulworth Castle (see page 116). When George III was passing through this area in 1788 on his way to Weymouth for his annual holiday, he was invited to come and see the chapel. As he entered, fifteen Weld children sang 'God Save the King'. This was *before* the passing of the Catholic Relief Act of 1791, so strictly speaking this was an illegal act of defiance – though of course it was not intended as such.

Our Lady Queen of Martyrs and St Ignatius, Chideock (1872)
Hidden by trees, this is difficult to find. Built, designed and decorated by Charles Weld himself, this has been called 'one of the most idiosyncratic and personal statements of Catholic faith in the country.' It contains a relic of the True Cross, and the hair shirt of Thomas More.

Church of the Annunciation, Charminster Road, Bournemouth (1906–7)
This church was built by none other than the young Giles Gilbert Scott, who also designed Liverpool's Anglican Cathedral, Waterloo Bridge, Battersea Power Station and the old-fashioned

red Post Office telephone kiosks. John Betjeman describes this church in Bournemouth as 'a brilliantly original design in brick.'

ABBEYS AND CHURCHES LOST OR DESTROYED

Dorset once had more abbeys and churches, but many were wantonly destroyed by Henry VIII. Others have been abandoned or put to other uses. These include:

Cerne

The only remaining part of the abbey at Cerne, traditionally founded by St Augustine, is an impressive gatehouse door. However, its tithe barn also survives.

Abbotsbury

Here there was a thriving Benedictine monastery, but all that remains of it are ruins, a chapel, and – like Cerne – a tithe barn, which was used to splendid effect in a film of *Far From the Madding Crowd*. The barn almost certainly made a useful hiding-place for smugglers to store their goods.

Bindon

The ruins of the old Cistercian Bindon Abbey are now part of a private country house. There is a traditional Dorset tale that the twelve bells of Bindon Abbey were stolen at night, and now hang in the churches of Wool, Coombe, and Fordington. A rhyme sums it up:

> Wool streams and Combe wells,
> Fordington cuckolds stole Bindon bells.

Forde

Forde Abbey is now a beautiful country mansion, which incorporates the ruins inside.

Milton

Milton Abbey still has its choir and transepts in use, but the site of the old abbey is now transformed into a successful independent school. The parish church at Milton is now deep below a man-made lake.

Shaftesbury

In the Middle Ages this great abbey, founded by Alfred the Great in AD 888, became fabulously rich as a result of the constant stream of visiting pilgrims. It was said that if the Abbess of Shaftesbury were to marry the Abbot of Glastonbury, any child born to them would be richer than the King of England himself. The abbey here was 350ft long (106m) and had an immense spire visible from all over the Blackmore Vale. Tragically, it was razed to the ground at the time of the Dissolution of the Monasteries.

Tyneham

Like all the rest of the village, the church of St Mary the Virgin was left abandoned in 1943, in order to provide a training ground for troops preparing for D-Day (see page 147.)

SURPRISING DECORATIONS

John the Baptist, Bere Regis

There are so many memorable carvings in both wood and stone in this church that it is impossible to mention them all here. The magnificent fifteenth-century timber roof is one of the glories of Dorset, showing the twelve apostles. But it is well worth looking at the stone capitals near the Turberville window – one showing a man with toothache (see p. 54).

St Mary, Durweston

The church contains a wonderfully preposterous fifteenth-century carving of St Eloy, patron saint of blacksmiths. It shows the saint shoeing a horse; in a manner only a saint could do – he has detached one of the horse's legs, and holds it in his left hand while he hammers the horse-shoe on with his right. The bewildered beast stands on its remaining three legs!

St George, Fordington

A splendid early twelfth-century carving over the south door shows St George on horseback, fighting in the Battle of Antioch, 1098, in the first crusade. He is complete with halo, and his lance is skewering an enemy on the battlefield. Two soldiers kneel behind him with their hands raised up in prayer, having stuck their own spears in the ground. It is a beautifully preserved piece of Norman carving.

Norman carvings on capitals in Bere Regis parish church 'Man with Toothache' and 'Man with Headache'.

St Mary, Melbury Bubb

The Saxon font here is one of the oddest sights in Dorset – for it is upside down! No one knows why it is like this – but probably it has been this way for about 900 years. If you skew your head round, you can make out a superb carving of a deer, with huge antlers – his feet touching the top rim, and his antlers at the base. It may have been part of an earlier old Saxon shaft, pressed into its present use as an easy way of making a font. The Dorset County Museum in Dorchester now has a plaster replica, the right way up!

St Nicholas, Moreton

Moreton church, which suffered much bomb damage during the Second World War, has been rebuilt with a great deal of skill. The shattered windows have been replaced and it is believed that this is the only church in the world to have windows entirely of engraved glass. They are the work of Laurence Whistler.

St Michael, Over Compton

The Goodden family of Compton House have done much to decorate and extend St Michael's church. The most striking feature here is a life-size statue of Robert Goodden (1751–1828). He stands up in the family pew, wearing country clothes and leaning on his stick. On church festivals he is given a button-hole to wear, of whatever flower happens to be in season. Oddly, the statue was erected during the lifetime of Robert Goodden, and was boarded up for a few years, waiting for him to die!

St Mary, Turnworth

This church still has its medieval tower, built in about 1500, but the whole of the rest of the church was pulled down and rebuilt in 1869–70. Interestingly, Thomas Hardy, then aged twenty-nine, had a great part in designing it. Of special interest are the carvings on the capitals which Hardy himself drew for the masons to copy. In particular, notice a splendid little owl on the tower arch – which is typical of Hardy's style of drawing.

5

KINGS & QUEENS

When the Romans left Britain in the early fifth century, England was immediately invaded by Angles, Saxons and Jutes. Gradually, seven Saxon kingdoms were established – Wessex being one of them. In the course of time, a forceful king of Wessex, Egbert, managed to unite the whole of England under his rule. There were nineteen Kings of Wessex, from Cerdic (519–34) to Egbert (802–39).

Egbert of Wessex was the first Saxon king to be hailed as 'sole ruler of Britain', in about AD 825. Egbert was then followed by sixteen more Saxon kings, the last of which was Harold II, killed at the Battle of Hastings in 1066.

According to tradition, the early Saxon leaders were descended from the pagan god Woden – whose name is forever remembered every week in the name 'Wednesday'.

As Queen Elizabeth II is descended from Cerdic, the House of Windsor must also claim to be distantly descended from Woden!

Three kings of Wessex who were older brothers of Alfred the Great are buried in Dorset churches: Ethelbald (858–60) and Ethelbert (860–5) are buried in Sherborne Abbey; and Ethelred I (866–71), is buried in Wimborne Minster.

King Alfred himself, aged about 20, attended the funeral of his older brother Ethelred in Wimborne Minster. At that funeral, he must have realised what an enormous task he was inheriting, to take up the kingship of Wessex.

Edward, King and Martyr (975–8), a great-great-grandson of Alfred the Great, was buried first at Wareham, and then at Shaftesbury. His curious story is told opposite. . . .

THE MURDER OF A TEENAGE KING

Fifteen-year-old Saxon King Edward was murdered in Dorset on 18 March 978, probably on the orders of his stepmother, Elfrida, when he went to visit her at Corfe Castle. Her stepmotherly motive was the quite natural one of wanting to place her own son Ethelred (the Unready) on the throne.

When the teenage king arrived on horseback he was being offered a goblet of wine when an assassin stabbed him. He fell from the saddle, but his foot became stuck in a stirrup as his horse galloped off, dragging him along the ground until he finally fell, lifeless into a small stream. His body was taken to a nearby cottage where a poor old blind woman lived, and he was covered with a rough cloth. During that night, the cottage was filled with a strange light, and miraculously, the blind woman's sight was restored. It is said that the church of St Edward at Corfe is built on the site of her cottage.

Edward was buried first at Wareham, but when miracles occurred at his burial spot, he began to be regarded as a saint and martyr. It was then decided to take his sacred body to be reburied in Shaftesbury Abbey.

DORSET'S MOST EXTRAORDINARY FUNERAL PROCESSION

The removal of the body of Edward, King and Martyr, from Wareham to Shaftesbury was the occasion of an astonishingly solemn, slow-moving procession of churchmen and nobles. The royal corpse was accompanied by the Earl of Mercia, the Bishop of Sherborne, the Abbess of Wilton and all her nuns. All these, and many high-ranking nobles of Wessex with their retinues and armed men, were led by none other than Dunstan, the Archbishop of Canterbury, who himself later became a saint.

With slow pomp, the prestigious company moved through fields and country lanes taking seven whole days to travel the 24-mile distance from Wareham, and then the king's body was laid to rest in a grave prepared for it near the high altar of Shaftesbury Abbey. Dorset has never witnessed a more impressive funeral than this. (For what happened next see the chapter Bones & Burials, page 14).

ENGLISH MONARCHS AND DORSET:
1066 TO THE TWENTY-FIRST CENTURY

William the Conqueror (reigned 1066–87)
The Conqueror abolished Dorset's only cathedral when he reorganised the pattern of English dioceses. Sherborne ceased to be the seat of a bishop, and Salisbury (Old Sarum) gained the status of being a cathedral city.

King Richard I ('The Lionheart') (reigned 1189–99)
Before he left England to go on the Third Crusade, Richard gave his brother – the future King John – the entire royal revenues of six English counties, Dorset being one of them – the others were Cornwall, Devon, Somerset, Derby and Nottingham.

King John (reigned 1199–1216)
King John was fond of Dorset, especially enjoying hunting here. Bere Manor House was from early times one of the royal manors (hence the word 'Regis' – 'of the king'), and King John stayed there on sixteen occasions between 1204 and 1216. He built a hunting lodge at Bere Regis but the exact site is unknown.

King Henry III (reigned 1216–72)
Henry III ordered the sheriff of Dorset to cause 'an image of a queen' to be cut in marble and carried to the nunnery of Tarrant Keynston, there to be placed over the tomb of his sister, the late Queen of Scots (see next item).

Queen Joan of Scotland (lived 1210–38)
King Henry III must have been shocked and deeply saddened by the death of his sister, Joan – just three years younger than himself, and aged only twenty-eight when she died. His order for 'an image of a queen' to be cut was carried out – though the workers did not feel it necessary to make it a likeness.

Joan had married King Alexander II of Scotland, and had been presented with the nunnery at Tarrant Crawford by Bishop Richard Poore, who had recently re-founded it. She died young, and was buried here shortly after she had received Bishop Poore's gift.

King Edward I (reigned 1272–1307)

Edward I gave Lyme its royal charter in 1284 – and from then the town enjoyed its extra title – Lyme Regis.

King Edward II (reigned 1307–27)

Edward II was held prisoner in Corfe Castle before being taken to Berkeley Castle to be murdered. He was guilty of being a homosexual.

King Edward VI (reigned 1547–53) and 'The Remedy Oak'

Edward VI was Henry VIII's young son who came to the throne, aged just nine. He was still just a young teenager (fourteen) when he came to visit Poole in 1551. Unfortunately the plague broke out when he was there, so he was hurriedly moved to Wilton House, near Salisbury. While he was there, a hunt was arranged for his entertainment at Cranborne Chase, and the young king rode out to watch the fun.

According to local tradition, Edward somehow got separated from the main party and stopped for a while to rest under an enormous oak tree near the Dorset village of Verwood. When the local inhabitants heard that the king was nearby they thronged around him, particularly asking him to 'touch' them for any illnesses they might have. Superstitiously, they believed that an anointed monarch was so sacred that even to be touched by a king or queen would cure them, particularly if they suffered from the 'King's Evil', a form of tuberculosis of the skin. So, to oblige the country folk, the young King Edward, sitting under the ancient oak, duly 'touched' his Dorset subjects.

The Remedy Oak, the tree under which Edward VI 'cured for evil'.

The oak still survives – a huge tree thought to be more than 800 years old – and ever since that extraordinary day when Edward VI 'touched for evil' it has been known as 'The Remedy Oak'. Beside it, a brass plaque records the event. In 1990 the East Dorset District Council bought the tree for £1, and in 2010 it replaced the cables which are needed to hold up this aged and now hollow tree.

If the story of the Remedy Oak seems far-fetched, it's worth remembering that over the centuries very many English and French kings regularly 'touched' for sickness. Edward the Confessor (1042–66) seems to have begun the practice in England, though French kings had done so for centuries before him. Charles II (1660–85) touched nearly 24,000 people in the first four years of his reign, and gave special coins to give to those he touched – known as 'touch pennies'. Queen Anne (1702–14) was the last monarch to keep up the practice in England – among those she touched was Dr Samuel Johnson, as a toddler. He vaguely remembered her.

Katherine of Aragon (first wife of Henry VIII)
Katherine stayed at Shaftesbury Abbey on her way from Plymouth to London to marry firstly Prince Arthur, and then Prince Henry – later, as Henry VIII, to be the destroyer of all abbeys in Britain.

King Charles II (reigned 1660–85)
After the Great Fire of London in 1666, Charles II was concerned to help the rebuilding programme, especially in the construction of the new St Paul's Cathedral. He ensured that Wren was not hindered in obtaining his supply of stone from Portland. The king made his demands known:

> There hath for many years past been great waste made of our stone in the Isle of Portland . . . in consideration of which, and the great occasion we have of using much of the said stone for the repair of St Paul's, our pleasure is, and we do by these presents will and require all persons whatsoever, that they forbear to transport any more stone from our Isle of Portland without the leave and warrant first obtained from *Dr Christopher Wren, surveyor of our works.*

Rebellion begins in Dorset
Lyme Regis was the scene of much excitement on 11 June 1685, when the thirty-six-year-old James Scott, 1st Duke of Monmouth,

landed there with a small army, intending to mount a rebellion against his uncle, King James II, and to claim the throne for himself. He was the illegitimate son of Charles II and Lucy Walter – much loved by his father and dreadfully spoilt and petted at court. On the death of his father, as a Protestant the Duke of Monmouth felt that he would be much more popular as a king than his Catholic uncle James II.

Enthusiasm he may have had in plenty, but his plans ran into serious difficulties. He desperately lacked horses, and sent out men to scour the countryside for them. Then two of his three ships, still carrying ammunition, were captured. And finally he lacked provisions. The duke was worried about feeding his growing army until his chaplain, the Revd Robert Ferguson, came up with an ingenious temporary solution. Ferguson told the duke that he would provide subsistence for one day for the entire army if only he would give him command of it for one minute. The puzzled duke agreed, whereupon the chaplain declared that the following day would be observed as a solemn fast, to ensure the success of the enterprise!

On 6 July, his army, nicknamed the 'pitchfork army' because of its pathetically ill-equipped forces, suffered a disastrous defeat at the Battle of Sedgemoor. The Duke of Monmouth stripped off his armour and galloped off into the night, leaving his ragged followers to be hacked to pieces.

A royal bastard hides in a ditch

A few miles to the north of Bournemouth is a popular pub called The Monmouth Ash – named after the dramatic moment when, a few days after the battle of Sedgemoor, the defeated Duke of Monmouth was found hiding in a ditch, covered in ferns and bracken under an ash tree. Desperately, the duke was trying to escape to the continent, and was heading for Poole. However, his luck ran out; he was spotted by a woman named Amy Farrant and the hunt was on.

A militiaman named Parkin caught sight of the duke's brown coat beneath some leaves in a ditch, and grabbed at it. The poor duke, terrified, gave himself up. In his pocket was the badge of the Order of the Garter, recipes for cosmetics, some forecasts by astrologers, and a number of weird charms to ward off evil. Sadly, these didn't

The Monmouth Ash, the tree and ditch where the hapless Duke of Monmouth was found after the Battle of Sedgemoor.

do him much good. Within a fortnight he was beheaded for treason.

King George II (reigned 1727–60)
When Blandford Forum was devastated by a terrible fire in 1731, which destroyed most of the town, King George II gave £1,000 to the disaster fund to help rebuild it.

George III (reigned 1760–1820) invents the seaside holiday
Until the end of the eighteenth century, holidays by the sea were simply unimaginable. It was the trend-setting idea of King George III to spend week upon week, year after year, at the seaside – and his chosen town was Weymouth. From then on, seaside holidays became immensely popular.

The king's brother, the Duke of Gloucester, had already taken a house on Weymouth seafront in the early 1780s, and the king,

Queen Charlotte, and their three eldest daughters spent six weeks at Gloucester Lodge in 1789. It was on 7 July that his majesty took his first dip in the sea. The novelist Fanny Burney, who was in charge of the queen's wardrobe, recorded the occasion: 'a machine (i.e. a bathing machine) follows the Royal one into the sea, filled with fiddlers, who play "God Save the King", as His Majesty takes his plunge.'

The king was delighted with the experience, and bought Gloucester Lodge and four other houses along the seafront. Subsequently, between 1789 and 1805, he came twelve times to Weymouth, usually staying for about six weeks at a time. His wife, poor Queen Charlotte, bearer of his fifteen children, hated it.

Today, Gloucester Lodge is the Gloucester Hotel, and the importance of George III's many visits to the town is forever demonstrated in the life-sized, brilliantly-painted, rather gaudy statue of the king on Weymouth's seafront promenade.

George III sitting on the Osmington Horse, a chalk hill figure 4 miles north of Weymouth, covering nearly an acre of ground.

George III dislikes Kingston Maurward

Those who are familiar with Kingston Maurward may be surprised to know that the original house, built by George Pitt, cousin of William Pitt the Elder, was originally built of brick. George III, visiting Kingston Maurward during one of his regular holidays in Weymouth, was not at all impressed. 'Brick, Mr Pitt, brick,' he kept on repeating – so much so that when the king had departed, poor Pitt, embarrassed and mortified, had his house entirely encased in Portland stone. It cost him a fortune but generations later, we can enjoy the elegant stone architecture – thanks to George III.

Princess Victoria visits Dorset

In July and August 1833, when she was aged fourteen, Princess (later Queen) Victoria was taken on a tour to visit the West Country, starting from the Isle of Wight, where her mother, the Duchess of Kent, rented Norris Castle at Cowes for the summer. The Princess went first to Southampton and Portsmouth, and then into Dorset and Devon.

Earlier, in 1832, Victoria had been taken through Warwickshire into Wales, travelling through Cheshire, Staffordshire, Derbyshire and Oxford. The two tours were designed to show Victoria the country over which she would soon reign – and also, of course, to show the princess to the people.

As is well known, Victoria kept a diary all her life – totalling 122 volumes. Sadly, at her death most of these were destroyed by her daughter, Princess Beatrice, but luckily, the volumes of the diary Victoria kept when she was a girl visiting Dorset still exist – the only volumes to have survived. Here are some typical extracts:

Monday, July 29. – I awoke at ¼ past 6 and got up at 7. At 8 we breakfasted. At 9 we went aboard the Emerald . . . She is to be towed by the Messenger steam-boat up to Weymouth. We passed Hurst Castle and the Needles. Poor Mamma began to be dreadfully sick soon after, which was a great pity and was a great drawback to any amusement. At about 1 I got some hot mutton chops which were very nice. It was very rough sometimes and poor Mamma suffered a good deal. We passed Lulworth Castle, the property of Mr. Weld. The coast was very pretty all the way. We passed the Isle of

Portland. About ½ past 3 we arrived at Weymouth where we received a <u>most</u> friendly and <u>civil</u> reception. The mayor and corporation walked before our carriage. I forgot to mention that <u>dear, sweet</u> Dashy [Victoria's pet dog] came with us. He was rather frightened.

The hotel is pretty good. At 5 we drove in flys through the streets and went into the library and shell shop. We came home at a ¼ past 6. At 7 we all dined. After dinner there was a pretty illumination. It is a pretty place and the houses are well built. It is very close to the sea and the sands are very fine. There is a statue raised to the memory of George the 3d who passed 6 weeks here almost every summer. I stayed up until ½ past 9. I was soon in bed, but the intense heat prevented my sleeping.

Princess Victoria and her mother then went on to Melbury House:

Wednesday, July 31. – I awoke at 7, and got up at 8. The house is old but comfortable. At ½ past 9 we all breakfasted. We then went upstairs and I wrote some letters and worked a little. At about ½ past 1 we lunched. After luncheon Lady Caroline brought her little parroquet down which is so tame that it comes on to your hand. It held up its foot to Lady Caroline's mouth to be kissed and kissed her. I said 'Very good, very good' and 'oh dear, oh dear', etc. etc. . . . We then went up a tower and the shape of Mamma's and my foot was cut on the leads. [The outline of the two feet are still there, marked on the roof at Melbury House.]

Thursday 1st August. – I awoke at 7 and got up at ¼ past 7. At 8 we breakfasted. All the Ladies breakfasted with us. At a ¼ past 9 we left Melbury. We went in the same way as we came as to carriages I mean. We passed through Beaminster where we were most <u>enthusiastically</u> received. The houses were ornamented with flags and flowers, and arches of flowers where [sic] erected across the streets.

Thomas Hardy's mother sees Princess Victoria pulled down by her skirts

In 1833, Thomas Hardy's mother, Jemima Hand, aged twenty, was a servant-girl working in Maiden Newton. She managed to get a glimpse of Princess Victoria on her tour of Dorset. She noted that when the crowds cheered the fourteen-year-old princess, she stood up in the carriage to acknowledge their welcome – but her mother 'promptly pulled her down into her seat by her skirts.'

Edward VII's Love-Nest in Bournemouth

Edward VII (reigned 1901–10) was notorious for his many mistresses – and one of the most famous was Lillie Langtry, 'the Jersey Lily', whom Edward first met in 1877, when he was still the Prince of Wales. She was the daughter of the Dean of Jersey, and was already married when he met her. With the prince's support and encouragement she went on the stage and became a rich and successful actress.

Edward bought a house for her in Bournemouth, a love-nest where he could visit her in relative privacy. Today it is a popular hotel and restaurant, Langtry Manor Hotel, but there are still tell-tale souvenirs of its royal past – including an enormous more-than-king-size genuine Jacobean four-poster bed! On the landing there is a small hatch-door looking down into the dining room, specially made so that Edward could look down on the guests before coming down for dinner.

Also, bold letters carved on the minstrels' gallery in the restaurant itself proclaim: THEY SAY – WHAT SAY THEY? LET THEM SAY. In other words, Edward and his mistress Lillie Langtry couldn't care less what gossip-mongers were saying about them.

Prince Charles's village in Dorset in the twenty-first century

Just outside Dorchester is one of the most remarkable 'villages' in the country – Poundbury. It owes its existence to Prince Charles, whose keenness for architecture has been a lifetime's passion. It is an experimental new village – or urban extension – on the outskirts of Dorchester and it has been built according to the strongly-held ideals of Prince Charles. It has links with what is known as 'New Urbanist' principles, which support the idea of 'walkable neighbourhoods'. The houses are interestingly individualistic, with a fascinating feeling of the past, though still modern and somehow 'different'.

The overall plan was developed in the 1980s by the European architect Leon Krier, and the actual construction began in

October 1993. It was expected that the four-plan phases would be developed over 25 years, with an ultimate total of 2,500 dwellings and a population of about 6,000. Andrew Brownsword, a greetings card entrepreneur, has sponsored the £1 million development of the market hall at Poundbury – Brownsword Hall – designed by John Simpson and based on earlier traditional designs, especially the seventeenth-century Market House in the Cotswold town of Tetbury, near the prince's home at Highgrove.

Quietly, over the years, Prince Charles has monitored Poundbury's development, and has involved himself personally in every aspect of this unusual 'royal village'. Talk to the 'villagers' and they will tell you how Charles keeps popping into their lives. Visitors to Dorchester should visit Poundbury. Designed by a future king, and defying description, Poundbury will live on as Dorset's royal village for many centuries to come.

6

HARDY & WESSEX

There were three phases in Thomas Hardy's life: in the first thirty years of his life he was educated in Dorchester and then worked as an architect in Dorset and London. During the next twenty-five years he was a novelist. Finally, in his last thirty-three years, he was a poet.

Hardy's single-minded ambition to be a writer was intense. From the age of thirty-two he earned his living entirely from his novels – mostly based on his memories of Dorset and the stories he gathered from his beloved 'Wessex'. In one ten-year period he wrote no fewer than seven full-length novels, and at the end of his life he had written 15 novels, 55 short stories, 2 plays and almost 1,000 poems.

HARDY'S FIVE HOMES IN DORSET

First Home: 'Hardy's Cottage' at Higher Bockhampton
Hardy's Cottage, now owned by the National Trust, provides the perfect starting-point for looking at Hardy's world. The cottage is superbly picturesque, but the real interest is that it was here on 2 June 1840 that Thomas Hardy was born.

The cottage was built in 1801 by his great-grandfather, John Hardy of Puddletown, and it was the home of his grandfather, Thomas Hardy, and then of his father, also Thomas Hardy. All these were builders and stone-masons who plied their trade around the immediate area and carved some of their work around the cottage.

At birth, Thomas Hardy was thought to be still-born and was lying neglected on the table when fortunately the midwife thought she saw a slight movement. Luckily, the little newborn child was helped to survive, frail though he was.

Hardy's Cottage, as drawn by Thomas Hardy himself. (Courtesy of Dorset County Museum)

He lived in this cottage throughout his childhood, teenage years, and returned here to write his early novels. His link with the place continued throughout his life, as his younger sister Kate remained here until her death in 1940.

Second Home: 'Riverside Villa' in Sturminster Newton

'Riverside Villa' was the first home of Thomas Hardy and his first wife, Emma. They lived here for two years, from 1876 to 1878, renting it as a brand-new semi-detached house overlooking the River Stour. Unfortunately it is not possible to visit Riverside Villa, but its position can be appreciated by walkers in this tranquil area, just upstream from Sturminster's wonderfully photogenic mill.

The couple, in their mid-thirties, had been married for only two years, and must have still be hoping for children – though it became an increasing sadness to Hardy that none came. Nevertheless, he described the two years they spent at Riverside as 'our happiest time' and it was here, in the upstairs front room with a view over the river, that Hardy wrote *The Return of the Native*.

Somewhat inexcusably, the plaque on 'Riverside' was originally placed on the wrong house! It should have been on the more northerly of the two houses – furthest from the recreation ground. Hardy himself had pointed out exactly where he had written *The Return of the Native*. The confusion arose from interpreting the position of a monkey-puzzle tree Hardy had planted. Fortunately, the plaque is now on the right house – but so distant from the footpath that you need a pair of binoculars to read it.

Third Home: 'Llanherne' in Wimborne Minster

Llanherne at 16 The Avenue, Wimborne, was the next Dorset home of Emma and Thomas. They moved into it on 25 June 1881, and the Blue Plaque on the wall states 'Thomas Hardy lived here 1881–1883'. It is something of a surprise to find such a suburban residence linked with Hardy, as he is so firmly linked with isolated rural scenes. Llanherne is a good, solid brick-built house with a slate roof, six rooms upstairs, and a sitting room, dining room, kitchen and conservatory downstairs. The lavatory in Hardy's time would have been in a little shed in the garden – and of course there was no bathroom, as was typical for a house built in 1872.

On their first night there, in mid-summer, Emma and Thomas sat in the conservatory and gazed at an extraordinary sight – the passing of Tebbutt's Comet. Hardy's imagination was always stirred by the mysterious workings of the universe, and this moment, when he and Emma stared up at the skies together, must have been at the back of his mind as he was preparing to write *Two on a Tower*, published the following year, in 1882. It is a story of an older woman and a younger man of inferior social standing – a situation which reflected his own relationship with Emma.

Wimborne Minster is within easy walking distance of Llanherne and Hardy attended many services there. He wrote at least two poems directly inspired by the minster, one of which refers to the 'Jack' – a small painted wooden figure of a soldier on one of the outside walls of the tower, who smartly hits two bells to tell of the passing hours. The poem is entitled 'Copying Architecture in an old Minster'. In it, Hardy wryly remarks:

> Just so did he clang here before I came,
> And so will he clang when I'm gone . . .

The other, a humorously macabre poem, 'The Levelled Churchyard', refers to the churchyard surrounding Wimborne Minster, which had just been tidied up to present a neat uncluttered lawn instead of a sprawling set of tombstones. In this, Hardy imagines the bones of the dead all jumbled up together:

> We, late-lamented, resting here,
> Are mixed to human jam,

And each to each exclaims in fear,
'I know not which I am!'

The wicked people have annexed
The verses on the good.
A roaring drunkard sports the text
Teetotal Tommy should!

Where we are huddled none can trace
And if our names remain
They pave some path or porch or place
Where we have never lain!

Here's not a modest maiden elf
But dreads the final Trumpet
Lest half of her should rise herself,
And half some sturdy strumpet!

Hardy had been suffering from ill-health as he and Emma settled into Llanherne, but he revived his strength here in Wimborne, and continued to write and collect Dorset stories for future works.

Hardy was in his early forties when living in Wimborne. Later in life, in a typical mood of melancholy nostalgia, he wrote of the lime trees of The Avenue:

They are great trees, no doubt, by now
That were so thin in bough –
That row of limes –
When we housed there, I'm loth to reckon when.
The world has turned so many times,
So many, since then.

Fourth Home: Shire-Hall Place, Dorchester

Shire-Hall Place no longer exists, but it had been the house of the headmaster of Dorset County School in Dorchester. It was a long, dark, rambling building running along the back of houses on the north side of High West Street. It stood on the site of the present Dorset County Council's health clinic. A local townsman is quoted as describing the house: 'He have but one window and she do look into Gaol Lane.' Thomas and Emma lived here from June 1883 to June 1885, waiting for Max Gate to be completed.

Shire-Hall Place was in the very middle of Dorchester, within three minutes' walk of the museum.

Fifth Home: Max Gate, on the outskirts of Dorchester
Max Gate, on the outskirts of Dorchester, now owned by the National Trust, was Hardy's final home, where he lived for over forty years. He designed it himself, having bought a 1½-acre site high on open heathland. He paid what was then the vast sum of £450 for the site, which was owned by the Duchy of Cornwall. He entrusted the work of building it to his father and brother, which is said to have ruffled a few family feathers as Hardy himself insisted on supervising the work!

He and Emma moved there on 29 June 1885. She died in 1912, and in 1914 Hardy married his former secretary, Florence Dugdale. He continued to live in Max Gate with Florence until he died in 1928. Florence gave the contents of his study to the Dorset County Museum in Dorchester, where a replica of the study and many of his belongings can be seen. When Florence herself died, Hardy's sister Kate bought the house at auction, and when she died in 1940, she gave it to the National Trust – though it is still mainly a private home, with only the drawing room and the garden open to visitors.

In the garden visitors can see a 'Druid Stone' because Max Gate is built on the site of a Neolithic stone circle and was also a part of a Romano-British cemetery – circumstances which must have appealed greatly to Hardy. Also to be seen is a sundial which Hardy designed for himself – he was always intrigued by time, and referred to himself as 'a time-torn man'. Also in the garden is the pets' cemetery, where all his cats and dogs are buried, including the notorious 'Wessex', who would try to bite anyone who came to the house – all except Lawrence of Arabia!

Max Gate finally acquired a bathroom in 1920 – so, at the ripe old age of eighty, Hardy was able to have a bath in his own home at last.

Max Gate gets its name from Mack's Gate – an old Toll House on the Wareham Road on the outskirts of Dorchester. In fact it's on land owned by the Duchy of Cornwall – or more precisely, whoever happens to be the current Prince of Wales. It was Prince

Albert, the future King Edward VII, who, as Prince of Wales, agreed to lease whatever piece of land that Thomas Hardy might choose on Duchy of Cornwall property to build his home on. Hardy chose 'Mack's Gate'.

SEVEN OTHER HARDY ADDRESSES

It is tempting to think of Hardy as dwelling exclusively in Bockhampton or Max Gate – but in fact his life included several other locations, both as a young man and also when married to Emma. Other addresses were:

16 Westbourne Park Gardens, Bayswater, 1863–7, working as an architect for John Hicks.

3 Wooperton Street, Weymouth, 1869–70, working as an architect for G.R. Crickmay. At this time he was working on his second novel, *Desperate Remedies*.

St David's Villa, Hook Road, Surbiton, 1874–5, rented accommodation by Thomas and Emma after returning from their honeymoon in Rouen and Paris.

18 Newton Road, Westbourne Grove, Bayswater, 1875, moving here from Surbiton to be nearer to the centre of London.

West End Cottage in Swanage, 1875–6, in a cul-de-sac off Seymour Road. It was the home of 'an invalid captain of smacks and ketches.' Here Hardy finished *The Hand of Ethelberta*.

7 Peter Street, Yeovil – Thomas and Emma briefly lodged here in 1876, before moving to Sturminster Newton. The site is now taken by a car park.

1 Arundel Terrace, Trinity Road, Tooting ('The Larches') 1878–81, Thomas and Emma moved here to be once again nearer London life. However, Hardy's prolonged illness here led them to return to Dorset (Wimborne) in 1881.

For the last forty-two years of his life, Hardy lived at Max Gate – but he and Emma would regularly go each year to spend time in London for 'the season'. Sadly for Florence, he never took her to London for the season. Perhaps he was getting too old, but she – thirty-seven years his junior – would perhaps have dearly liked to have gone!

HARDY'S NOVELS – WHERE AND WHEN HE WROTE THEM

Aged 28 in 1868	*The Poor Man and the Lady*	written in Hardy's Cottage
Aged 31 in 1871	*Desperate Remedies*	written in Hardy's Cottage
Aged 32 in 1872	*Under the Greenwood Tree*	written in Hardy's Cottage
Aged 33 in 1873	*A Pair of Blue Eyes*	written in Hardy's Cottage
Aged 34 in 1874	*Far from the Madding Crowd*	written in Hardy's Cottage

(in 1874 Hardy married Emma Gifford, leaving the family cottage home)

Aged 36 in 1876	*The Hand of Ethelberta*	written in Swanage
Aged 38 in 1878	*The Return of the Native*	written in Sturminster Newton
Aged 40 in 1880	*The Trumpet-Major*	written in London
Aged 41 in 1881	*The Laodicean*	written in London
Aged 42 in 1882	*Two on a Tower*	written in Wimborne Minster
Aged 46 in 1886	*The Mayor of Casterbridge*	written in Shire-Hall Place, Dorchester
Aged 47 in 1887	*The Woodlanders*	written in Max Gate, Dorchester
Aged 51 in 1891	*Tess of the D'Urbervilles*	written in Max Gate
Aged 51 in 1891	*A Group of Noble Dames*	written in Max Gate
Aged 52 in 1892	*The Well-Beloved*	written in Max Gate
Aged 55 in 1895	*Jude the Obscure*	written in Max Gate

The publication of his last novel, *Jude the Obscure*, created instant uproar. The reviews were so virulent that Hardy gave up any attempt to write more novels. His relationship with Emma became tense and even more strained. From then on he concentrated on poetry, and published collections containing poems he had written over many years, and also new ones he was constantly producing. He wrote poems almost to the day he died. His only other major work after *Jude the Obscure* was the vast project on the Napoleonic Wars – *The Dynasts – An Epic Drama of the War with Napoleon in Three Parts, Nineteen Acts, and One Hundred and Thirty Scenes*.

SOME TERRIBLE REVIEWS OF *JUDE THE OBSCURE*

Hardy began to write his last novel, *Jude the Obscure*, in 1892 and it was published in 1895. His wife Emma was so shocked and horrified by it that she made a special journey to London to try to prevent its publication. However, her journey was in vain. The reception of *Jude* was overwhelmingly hostile. Here are some typical reviews:

'the reader closes this book with a feeling that a huge pall has blotted out all the light of humanity.'
'A titanically bad book.'
'Mr Hardy running mad in right royal fashion.'
'Dangerously near to farce.'
'Jude the Obscene.'
'A shameful nightmare.'
'A man must be a fool to deliberately stand up to be shot at.'
'Too deplorable a falling-off from Mr Hardy's former achievements to be reckoned with at all.'
'What has Providence done to Mr Hardy, that he should rise up in the arable land of Wessex and shake his fist at his Creator?' (Edmund Gosse)

The Bishop of Wakefield boasted that he had thrown his copy into the fire.

An American woman writer declared, 'When I finished the story I opened the windows and let in the fresh air.'

HARDY AND GOD

Much of the hostility towards Hardy was the result of his anguished thoughts about God. Aged nineteen when *On the Origin of Species* was published, he found it increasingly impossible to reconcile a world of tragedy and suffering with a God of love. He remained a church-goer to the end of his days, but his poetry contains some extraordinary ways of describing the deity:

The President of the Immortals
The Spinner of the Years
The Immanent Will that stirs and urges everything
one called God, though by some the Will, or Force, or Laws,
And vaguely, by some the Ultimate Cause.

The Great Face behind
Some vast imbecility
That Which some enthrone
The Inscrutable
The Hid
The Immanent Doer That doth not know

The essence of Hardy's bitter view of God can been seen in many of his poems – typically, *New Year's Eve*, dated 1906. Hardy imagines God having no explanation of why he created the world, and having no ethic or purpose. The Deity weaves the future 'in his unweeting way.'

HARDY AND THE HANGING OF MARTHA BROWNE

Hardy was aged sixteen and had just started his apprenticeship with John Hicks in Dorchester, when an event took place that would haunt his mind for the rest of his life – the public hanging of a young woman in front of Dorchester Prison.

Martha Browne, a former servant-girl, had found her husband in bed with another woman. In the ensuing quarrel he lashed out at her with a whip, and she had responded by smashing his skull with a wood-axe. Nobody believed her story that her husband had been kicked to death by a horse, and she was sentenced to be hanged.

An estimated crowd of between three and four thousand people flocked to the prison gates, and Britain's principal hangman, William Calcraft, was brought in specially to officiate. He was noted for his 'short drops' – which caused most of his victims to die a slow and agonising death.

As a curious teenager, Hardy was determined to get a good view of this spectacle, and managed to climb up a tree very near the gallows. He saw every detail, including the fact that Calcraft initially forgot to tie a cord round Martha's dress so that her legs would not be exposed (Victorian modesty!).

Martha Browne was the last woman to be publicly hanged in Dorset. Naturally, the scene made an unforgettable impression on Hardy. He described it and remembered it to the end of his days. It filled his imagination as he wrote *Tess of the D'Urbervilles*, and some of his biographers have quoted Hardy's eerily erotic description, noting 'what a fine figure she showed against the sky as she hung in the misty rain, and how the tight black silk gown set off her shape as she wheeled half round and back.'

AND ANOTHER HANGING SEEN AT A DISTANCE

Hangings were still regarded as a kind of public entertainment in Hardy's earlier years. He describes how one morning he was at breakfast in the cottage at Bockhampton when he remembered that a hanging was due to take place at 8.00 a.m. He quickly grabbed the family telescope and hurried out to a spot where he knew he could see the gallows – even though it was 3 miles distant.

The sun was lighting up the scene by the prison and just as Hardy put the telescope to his eye, the clock struck eight and he saw the figure of the victim drop downwards to his fate. Hardy was so shocked that he almost dropped the telescope. He wrote that he 'seemed alone on the heath with the hanged man, and crept homeward wishing he had not been so curious.'

Hardy's mind was filled with events and stories, legends and memories, and he even ransacked newspapers and magazines for curious episodes that he could use in his novels and stories. In *The Withered Arm* – one of his 'Wessex Tales' – he makes use of the old superstition that physical deformity was a result of witchcraft, and could be cured by touching the neck of a newly-hanged man.

HARDY'S WESSEX

As a result of Hardy's writings, 'Wessex' has been given a new lease of life as a place-name, after centuries of being merely a half-remembered relic of bygone Saxon times, like Mercia. To many, the area may be somewhat vague, but Hardy himself had a clear but personal view of what he meant by Wessex:

Lower Wessex	Devon
Mid Wessex	Wiltshire
North Wessex	Berkshire
Outer Wessex	Somerset
Upper Wessex	Hampshire
South Wessex	Dorset

Hardy invented more than 300 names for the towns, villages, roads, and even pubs throughout his re-envisaged Wessex – but he was always wary of being too precise about linking places to his fictional names.

He must have thought carefully about these names. Some show his wry sense of humour, such as *Sarcophagus College* in *Christminster* (Corpus Christi College or New College in Oxford). Other names show his love of history and old dialect words (*Shaston* and *Wintoncester* were older names for Shaftesbury and Winchester). His name for Portland, *The Isle of Slingers*, recalls the fact that the pebbles from Chesil Beach were notably used as sling-stones against the Romans.

HARDY'S DORSET

A selection of fictitious Dorset names. Hardy's names are in *italics*.

Abbot's Beach	Abbotsbury
Abbot's Cernel	Cerne Abbas
Anglebury	Wareham
Athelhall	Athelhampton
Broad Sidlinch	Sydling St Nicholas
Budmouth Regis	Weymouth & Melcombe Regis
Casterbridge	Dorchester
Chaldon	Chaldon Herring

Chalk Newton	Maiden Newton
Chaseborough	Cranborne
Corvsgate	Corfe Castle
Creston	Preston
Dead Man's Bay	West Bay
East Egdon	Affpuddle
East Quarriers	Easton
Eggar	Eggardon
Emminster	Beaminster
Estminster	Yetminster
Evershead	Evershot
Froom-Everard	West Stafford House
Greenhill	Woodbury Hill
Haggardon Hill	Eggardon Hill
Havenpool	Poole
Kingsbere	Bere Regis
King's Hintock	Melbury Osmund
Knapwater House	Kingston Maurward
Leddington	Gillingham
Longpuddle	Piddletrenthide and Piddlehinton
Lower Mellstock	Lower Bockhampton
Lulstead or *Lulwind Cove*	Lulworth Cove
Mai Dun	Maiden Castle
Martlott	Marnhull
Melstock	Stinsford
Middleton Abbas	Milton Abbas
Millpond St Jude	Milborne St Andrew
Nether Moynton	Owermoigne
Newland Buckton	Buckland Newton
Nuttlebury	Hazelbury Bryan
Oakford Fitzpiers	Okeford Fitzpaine
Overcombe	Sutton Poyntz
Pebble Beach	Chesil Beach
Port Bredy	Bridport
Pummery	Poundbury
Ringsworth Shore	Ringstead Bay
Sandbourne	Bournemouth
Shaston	Shaftesbury
Sherton Abbas	Sherborne
Shottsford Forum	Blandford Forum
Stourcastle	Sturminster Newton
Springham	Warmwell

Street of Wells	Fortuneswell
Sylvania Castle	Pennsylvania Castle
Tolchurch	Tolpuddle
Tranton	Tarrant Hinton
Upper Longpuddle	Piddletrenthide
Valley of the Great Dairies	The Frome Valley
Valley of the Little Dairies	The Blackmore Vale
Warborne	Wimborne
Weatherbury	Puddletown
Yalbury Wood	Yellowham Wood
Wellbridge	Wool

HARDY TRIVIA

Hardy's novels are translated into all European languages, Russian, Japanese, and many Indian languages. Hardy himself helped an early French translator, especially with curious Dorset dialect words.

Hardy wrote each novel with a different dip-pen. He inscribed the title on each pen as he finished a novel, and a collection of these pens are on the desk in his reconstructed study in Dorchester County Museum.

The statue of Hardy in Dorchester was unveiled on 2 June 1940, coinciding with the evacuation of the British Army from Dunkirk.

Hardy hated to be touched. He would walk down the middle of Dorchester High Street to avoid people brushing against him.

Five films were made of Hardy's novels in his own lifetime – but as he died in 1928, all these films, inevitably, were silent. Other films, of course, have been made since.

When, in old age, Hardy was taken around Dorset in a hired car, he would not allow the driver to go more than 25mph.

Cynthia Asquith was horrified to find that Hardy's monstrously-spoilt dog, Wessex, was allowed to walk about unchecked on the dinner-table 'contesting every single forkful of food on its way from my plate to my mouth.'

Hardy's last public speech was in July 1927, at the laying of the foundation stone of new buildings for Dorchester Grammar School for Boys.

Hardy's last words were to Eva Dugdale, his second wife's sister. Eva was a nurse, and had come to help him in his last days. His words: 'Eva, Eva, what is this?'

7

WORK & LEISURE

PORTLAND STONE –
'THE KING OF THE OOLITES'

Many people think of Dorset simply as a rural county, with an accent on farming, but there is one industry which makes Dorset a vibrant source of visual pleasure throughout the world – the incredible excellence of its Portland stone quarries A well-known expert on architecture once named Portland stone the 'king of the oolites' and called it 'arguably the finest building stone in England'. The point is that this stone has quite exceptional qualities to withstand weathering, and yet it is relatively easy to chisel and carve.

Sir Christopher Wren was so delighted with the excellent quality of Portland stone – which had been used by Inigo Jones for the Banqueting House in Whitehall – that he used over a million cubic feet of it for building St Paul's Cathedral and other city churches after the Great Fire of London. Such a demand gave a huge boost to quarrying at Portland. Special new piers had to be built, and for the first time a new quarry was opened up on land, away from the cliffs. Previously, all stone had been taken only from the cliff-sides.

We can see Dorset stone across the country, especially in our most important buildings. Here are just a few examples where Portland stone is used in Britain and throughout the world:

The Tower of London
St Paul's Cathedral
The Cenotaph
The Banqueting House
The British Museum
Somerset House
The Bank of England
The Mansion House

The National Gallery
Exeter Cathedral
Christchurch Priory
Cunard Building
Port of Liverpool Building
Cardiff Civic Centre
Nottingham Council House
The Queen's Gallery
Temple Bar in Paternoster Square
New BBC Broadcasting House
Condor House in London
Portcullis House in Westminster
The Tibetan Peace Garden at the Imperial War Museum
UN Building in New York
The National Gallery, Dublin
Casino Kursaal, Belgium
Belfast City Hall

All gravestones for British personnel killed in the First and Second World Wars are made out of Portland stone.

In 2008 a stunning piece of architecture was unveiled – the Armed Forces Memorial in Staffordshire. A circular structure 43 metres in diameter formed by Portland stone walls, it bears the names of over 16,000 service personnel who have died since the Second World War. 250 cubic metres of Portland stone were needed for this.

Nowadays, with new technology pioneered in Portland, the quarries are busier than ever, and the stone is in constant demand all over the world – being used in important architectural showpieces in places as far afield as Greece, Kuwait, Copenhagen and Japan.

In the summer of 1978, the 'Tower Stone' was unveiled in Victoria Square, Portland, by the Governor of the Tower of London. It was flanked by a party of Beefeaters in their colourful traditional uniform. The reason for this was to celebrate 900 years of Portland's recorded history, and to mark the fact that the Tower of London is the earliest national building to have used Portland stone.

'BUTTONY'

Compared with the Herculean work of the quarrymen of Portland, buttony was a much more genteel occupation – a cottage industry in Dorset, carried out mostly by women. But what on earth was 'Buttony'? Quite simply – it was the making of buttons!

Several parishes in Dorset, including Langton Matravers, were important centres of button-making. It was a popular local industry which had begun in Shaftesbury in 1650 by a man named Abraham Case. The first of these were 'High Tops' and 'Knobs', made on discs of horn from the Dorset Horned Sheep. As the industry grew, there were no fewer than 31 types of button, including 'Birdseye', 'Singleton', 'Old Dorset Mite', 'Crosswheel', 'Honeycomb', 'Yannels', 'Jams', 'Shirts' and 'Outsiders'.

At its peak, the trade annually brought in an estimated £12,000, and there were thousands of women working at home to produce buttons which were exported to Europe, Canada, Australia and America.

There were speciality Dorset buttons, chief of which was the Crosswheel, most often made in Langton Matravers. A small metal ring was covered in black or white material, and then with very fine stitches a pattern was embroidered on one side. A dozen or half-a-dozen of these were sewn onto colour-coded cards: pink for the best; yellow for the poorest quality.

Expert buttoners would make as many as a gross a day (144), for which they could be paid three shillings and sixpence. If the buttons were perfect they could even make three shillings and ninepence.

Catastrophically for Dorset buttony, Ashton's button-making machine was invented in 1850 and proudly exhibited at the Great Exhibition of 1851. As a consequence of this invention, the Dorset cottage industry collapsed virtually overnight, and sad to say it caused great distress among those families who depended on buttony for their living.

At government expense, many Dorset button-makers were helped to emigrate to Canada and Australia.

STRAW-MILLINERY

Another almost forgotten cottage industry in Dorset was the making of straw-bonnets – which were extremely fashionable throughout the nineteenth century and well into the twentieth. Special ivory tools were needed for splitting and flattening straw, and the bonnet-makers would then weave the pieces of straw into patterns. It was a skill that could be taught to women who were handicapped in some way, perhaps being crippled or deaf. The last straw-bonnet maker of Langton Matravers was Louise Bower – known as 'Deaf Lou'.

When the young Princess Victoria toured Dorset with her mother in 1833, she was presented with two bonnets from Hixon's Straw-plait Shop at No. 1, Sea-side, Weymouth. One of these bonnets was made by a Swanage woman, and the other by a woman from Langton Matravers.

When bonnets went out of fashion, straw-workers continued their skills by making straw table-mats.

PRICKLE-MAKERS

In other words, 'basket-makers'! Yet another cottage industry, and again one that could be done even by blind people or those who were too physically handicapped to engage in other trades. There was always a need for baskets and also for lobster-pots on the Dorset coast, and 'prickle-makers' were valued members of the community, earning their living by making baskets and containers of all shapes and sizes, using locally-grown osiers or willows.

Lobster pots and prickle-makers, a former thriving Dorset cottage industry.

The tombstone of a nineteenth-century basket-maker, 'Blind George' (George Corben), can be seen in Langton Old Cemetery. He was the inspiration for a popular novel, *Blind Jem and His Fiddle* by Mary E. Palgrave, published in 1884 by the SPCK and recently republished in 2009 by Barnes and Wallis. Poor old Blind George had lost his sight as a toddler, having suffered from smallpox. Neverthelesss, he led a useful life making 'prickles'.

'STABBED WITH A BRIDPORT DAGGER'

Now that the death penalty in England has long been abolished, the phrase 'stabbed with a Bridport dagger' is hardly remembered – but in former times everyone knew that a 'Bridport dagger' meant the hangman's rope!

The point is, Bridport was famed for its hempen goods, supplying ropes and cables for the Royal Navy in times when every ship needed hundreds of yards of rope for hoisting its sails. Even as long ago as the fifteenth century, Henry VII decreed that all the hemp grown in a 5-mile radius of Bridport was to be reserved exclusively for the use of the navy.

The width of Bridport's streets and the layout of its rope-walks remind visitors of Bridport's former local industry. Much space was needed. As rope was being made, one end of a piece of hemp was fastend to a spindle, with the handle usually turned by a boy, while the rope-maker carried the rest of the hemp wound round his body. He would walk backwards, pulling out the hemp and feeding it out to the spindle.

Donkeys would be used for the heavy work of pulling completed lengths of rope to be polished.

Today the hugely important Dorset industry of rope-making has vanished, but tourists can enjoy the town's museum in South Street showing details of Bridport's once-world-famous industry. There are even some examples of the knots formerly used by hangmen.

A FEW MILLION SILKWORMS

Silk-production is still thriving in Dorset. The only silk farm left in Britain is still producing its skeins of silk at Lullingstone Silk Farm near Sherborne. In fact, this farm breeds between three and four million silkworms annually.

Traditionally, Lullingstone provides silk for royal occasions, beginning with a request by Queen Mary – the consort of King George V – to provide silk for the coronation of her son, George VI. In more recent times, Lullingstone has produced silk for the weddings of Prince Charles and Princess Diana in 1981 and of Prince Andrew and Sarah Ferguson in 1986.

NODDING DONKEYS

Not many people immediately associate Dorset with oil-production, so they are surprised to learn that:

Dorset lies above Europe's largest onshore oil field.

It is operated by BP from Wytch Farm, in the vicinity of Poole harbour.

It has the world's oldest continuously pumping well – which has been going since the early 1960s.

It has the world's longest drill (5 miles), ending under Bournemouth pier.

At its peak production in 1993, the oil field produced 110,000 barrels per day.

In 2002 it was estimated that the field contained reserves of 64.4 million tonnes of oil.

This area under Dorset also contains an estimated 4.73 million tonnes of natural gas liquids, and 1.42 billion cubic metres of natural gas.

The oil is piped 57 miles from Wytch Farm via Fawley to a terminal at Hamble for export by tanker.

The natural gas (methane) is piped to Sopley, north of Christchurch, for use in the natural gas supply network.

Because this is an Area of Outstanding Natural Beauty, the gathering centre and most of the well sites are hidden by trees. Just a few 'nodding donkeys' can be seen from afar – that is, the constantly moving tops of the pumps, which look like the heads of donkeys.

THE FIRST EVER SCOUT CAMP – ON BROWNSEA ISLAND IN 1907

The most important leisure event ever to take place in Dorset took place in the first week of August 1907, on Brownsea Island. It was, of course, the first Scout camp, organised as an experiment for twenty-one boys 'of different social backgrounds'. This 'experiment' led to the foundation of the Scout Movement, now enjoyed by millions of girls and boys throughout the world. Here is an account of that extraordinary week in Dorset.

The origins of the Scout Movement lie in Colonel Baden-Powell's brilliant success in the Defence of Mafeking during the second Boer War. His success in holding the town for 217 days, from October 1899 to May 1900, made him a national hero. His idea to organise a camp for boys must have thrilled those lucky enough to take part.

During the Siege of Mafeking, Baden-Powell had been impressed by the courage and resourcefulness of a group of boys, the Mafeking Cadets, aged twelve to fifteen, who acted as messengers. He wrote a best-selling book, *Aids to Scouting for NCOs and Men*, and decided it would be a good idea to set up a new youth organisation, based on scouting skills.

Brownsea Island was the ideal site, covering 460 acres of woodland and open areas. It is just a short ferry distance from Poole, yet it provides isolation from intrusive snoopers and press reporters. Baden Powell had visited it as a boy, and now he was lucky to be given the use of the island by the owner, Charles van Raalte.

Twenty-one boys took part: eleven from Eton and Harrow, who were asked to pay £1 for the week's camp; seven from the Bournemouth Boys' Brigade and three from the Poole Boys' Brigade, who were charged 3s 6d.

The Scout Movement had not yet begun, so the boys had no uniform shirts. However, they were given khaki scarves and brass fleur-de-lis badges – the first ever use of the Scout emblem. They also wore a coloured knot on their shoulder to show their patrols: green for Bulls, blue for Wolves, yellow for Curlews, and red for Ravens. Patrol Leaders carried a staff with a flag depicting the patrol animal or bird.

After passing tests on knots, tracking and the national flag, the boys were then given another brass badge – a scroll with the words 'Be Prepared', to wear below the fleur-de-lis. The programme of events had a different theme on each day:

Day 1 Preliminary
Formation of patrols, distribution of duties, special instruction for Patrol Leaders, settle into camp.

Day 2 Campaigning
Camping skills, building huts, knots, fire-lighting, cooking, health and sanitation, endurance.

Day 3 Observation
Tracking, memorising details, deducing meaning from tracks and signs, training eyesight.

Day 4 Woodcraft
Study of animals and birds, plants, stars, stalking animals.

Day 5 Chivalry
Honour, code of the knights, unselfishness, courage, charity, thrift, loyalty, chivalry to women, doing a 'Good Turn' daily.

Day 6 Saving a life
From fire, drowning, sewer gas, runaway horses, panic, street accidents, etc. First Aid.

Day 7 Patriotism

History and deeds that won the Empire, our Navy and Army, flags, duties as citizens, marksmanship.

Day 8 Conclusion

Summary of the course, sports day.

From this humble but uniquely imaginative event in Dorset, the entire worldwide Scout Movement had its beginning. Centenary celebrations were held on Brownsea Island from 26 July to 4 August 2007, comprising four special camps: the Patrol Leaders' Camp for Scouts from the United Kingdom; the Replica Camp, which was a re-creation of the original camp of 1907; the Sunrise Camp, in which 300 Scouts from nearly every country in the world took part; and the New Centenary Camp, hosting Scouts from the UK and abroad, celebrating the start of the second century for Scouting – and demonstrating that it is possible for Scouts from all backgrounds and religions to come together in peace and friendship.

At the Sunrise Camp, at 8 a.m. on 1 August, exactly one hundred years from the start of the first 'experimental' camp, Scouts from all over the world renewed their Scout promise – focussing on the desire to make the world a better and more peaceful place.

Now, an area of 50 acres is permanently set aside for scout camping and activities on Brownsea Island. The Baden-Powell Outdoor Centre was opened on 14 September 2007 with a new camp reception, washrooms and toilet facilities. There is also a small Scouting museum.

BRITAIN'S FIRST MUNICIPAL ORCHESTRA

As a town, Bournemouth grew from a single wayside inn on bleak heathland in 1810 to a thriving and fashionable health resort of about 20,000 in the 1880s. In *Tess of the D'Urbervilles*, published in 1891, Thomas Hardy gave the new town the name of 'Sandbourne' – 'This fashionable watering-place . . . was like a fairy place suddenly created by the stroke of a wand, and allowed to get a little dusty.'

In 1876 the Italian Band – a group of sixteen Italian musicians who had served in the Italian Army – were performing regularly for the entertainment of residents and visitors. Led by a Signor Bertini and supported by the town authorities, they increased their number in 1892 to twenty-one musicians to form the first Corporation Military Band.

The Italian Band was so popular that the town council made a bold decision – to found a full orchestra. It would be the first municipal orchestra in the entire country and to run it they decided to invite none other than Dan Godfrey, an enormously famous bandsman of the day, known to all as one of Britain's leading musicians.

Dan Godfrey, however, had other commitments, and was not at all interested in settling down to found this new orchestra so far from the capital. He neglected even to reply to the offer.

Luckily for Bournemouth, however, his son, also named Dan, chanced to read his father's mail. The younger Dan Godfrey, aged twenty-four, had recently returned from South Africa, where he had been musical director of a touring opera company. He was young, newly married, ambitious, and urgently in need of a job. Swiftly he applied for the post offered to his father. And naturally enough – he got it!

This appointment was the beginning of the great success story that eventually led to the world-famous Bournemouth Symphony Orchestra.

Under Dan Godfrey's leadership, the orchestra played three times a day from Whitsun to October in the Winter Gardens. This was a large building which resembled the glass-houses at Kew. The musicians hated it because it was noisy when it rained, it was ferociously hot when it was sunny, and the foliage of the plants got in the way of their instruments. They called it 'The Glass-house' or 'The Greenhouse', or 'The Cucumber Frame' – this last name was a clever pun, because the designer of the Winter Gardens, Mr Cumber, had also designed buildings at Kew.

In 1929 the orchestra gained a brand-new venue for its performances when the Bournemouth Pavilion was opened.

In 1947, because of the poor acoustics of the Pavilion, it was decided to move to a refurbished building originally built as a bowling alley – the Winter Gardens. To everyone's delight, its acoustics proved to be amazingly good, and the orchestra gained worldwide fame under a succession of great conductors: Rudolf Schwarz, Constantin Silvestri, Charles Groves, and many more.

Despite protests and a petition with over 28,000 signatories, Bournemouth Borough Council demolished its once-famous Winter Gardens in 2003. The site is now a car park.

However, the Bournemouth Symphony Orchestra goes from strength to strength and now has its main concert hall in Poole.

DORSET TOURISM

Charles II declared that he never saw a finer country, either in England or out of it – but the Merry Monarch was never able to experience the vast and growing number of Dorset attractions which can now be enjoyed in the twenty-first century.

Tourism is arguably Dorset's major industry today. Its seaside towns attract millions, and the Jurassic Coast is famed throughout the world. In addition to its beautiful natural scenery and the charm of its picturesque villages, churches, and other old buildings, tourists are now overwhelmed by the choice of so many kinds of attractions – appealing to all tastes and ages.

Dorset visitors can see monkeys, swans, stingrays, sharks, castles, great houses, fine gardens, exhibitions ranging from dinosaurs to teddy-bears, tanks, butterflies, costumes, beer-making, working mills, farms, craft centres, steam trains, art galleries, model villages, and children can enjoy thousands of acres of country parks with adventure playgrounds . . . and much more besides.

Compare this range of opportunities with the naïve pride shown in Bournemouth's starchily-written first guide book – published in 1840. . . .

THE INVENTION OF THE BOARDING HOUSE AND 'PIC-NICS'

(From Bournemouth's First Guide Book – 1840)

... on spots where, before, the foot of man rarely pressed, but the lowly heath flower blossomed and faded in unnoticed solitude, where no sound was heard but the rustling of the rank grass and the wild shrub, as they waved in the light sea breeze – there a number of detached villas, each marked by distinct and peculiar architectural features, have sprung into existence, affording accommodation of varying extent, so as to be suited to the convenience of either large or small families, and adapted, some for extended, others for confined, establishments.

... for the appropriate accommodation of those numerous visitors who may prefer the retired and quiet mode of life ... the 'Belle-Vue Boarding House', situated close to the beach, has been fitted up with every regard to elegance and comfort, to which the attentions of Mrs Slidel, the conductress, are very conducive.

In addition to the ordinary advantages of such an institution, accommodations are provided for the more casual visitors, and parties preferring that delightful mode of recreation designated by the untranslateable term 'pic-nic', may here be provided with every requisite. A billiard table is attached to the establishment.

THE GREAT DORSET STEAM FAIR

The annual Great Dorset Steam Fair, held at Tarrant Hinton near Blandford Forum in early September, is now recognised as the leading show of its kind in the world. It displays far more than engines driven by steam – it is now regarded as Britain's most important National Heritage Show.

It has to be seen to be fully appreciated – but the following statistics may help to describe what has become Dorset's unique and most popular annual event:

Set in over 600 acres, it is one of Europe's largest outdoor events.

It has grown larger every year since the first Steam Fair in 1968.

200 working steam engines on display.

2,000 other working exhibits are put on show.

200,000 annual visitors enjoy watching demonstrations of steam engines driving ploughs, threshing, bailing, hauling, sawing planks – and much more.

It gathers together the world's largest collection of steam and vintage equipment.

Country crafts are on display, from thatching to cider-making. There are over 500 trade stands. Sheepdogs are seen at work, eagle and vulture shows, and there is also a music festival – and even authentic 1920s-style stage shows with genuine can-can dancers. All the fun of the annual Great Dorset Steam Fair!

Very sadly, the founder of this huge event, Michael Oliver MBE, died in 2009, but his infectious enthusiasm is sure to live on for as long as the giants of steam are still working.

DORSET OPERA

Starting in the 1970s, Dorset Opera has been successfully running what has been termed 'The world's foremost residential opera summer school'. The quality of the productions annually produces rave reviews – 'spectacular and magnificent' from the *Independent on Sunday*; 'nothing short of phenomenal!' from *Opera Magazine*; and 'consistently on a par with the UK's five main opera companies,' from *Opera Now.*

Using the Coade Theatre at Bryanston School for its productions, Dorset Opera Summer School gives an opportunity for between 50 and 80 people, ranging in age from sixteen to seventy – mostly under twenty-five – to take part in opera at the very highest standard.

The young people sing and work alongside world-renowned professional singers. Fees are astonishingly low for the residential course, and there are bursaries to help those who may need financial help.

Roderick Kennedy, who has sung leading parts in opera houses throughout the world as well as giving over 500 performances at the Royal Opera House, Covent Garden, has been the inspiration. For opera lovers, Dorset Opera is an annual highlight – and for youngsters who have the good fortune to take part, it can be a life-changing experience.

DORSET KNOB-THROWING

Hundreds of people come to the village of Cattistock on May Day Bank Holiday to watch or take part in the sport of Dorset Knob-Throwing. As everyone should know, Dorset Knobs are hard, dry, savoury biscuits special to the county, and those used at Cattistock are made by the Bridport-based firm of Moore's.

As at 2010 the record throws were: Ladies 20.2 metres, Gents 26.1 metres, and under-12s 18.5 metres. Anyone can throw, on payment to charity. Fun events also include knob-painting, knob-and-spoon races, knob darts, knob pyramid, and guess the weight of the Big Knob!

NETTLE-EATING

The World Nettle-Eating Championship must surely be one of Dorset's most extraordinary leisure events, growing in popularity year by year. It takes place at the Bottle Inn in the village of Marshwood a few miles north of Lyme Regis.

Competitive nettle-eating began as a result of a light-hearted bet in 1986 between two farmers about who had the longest stinging nettles in their fields. One of the farmers, Alex Williams, promised he would eat any nettle longer than his. He lost the bet – and courageously ate his challenger's lengthier nettle.

Since then, nettle-eating has developed into a world-famous sport, and the championship is held as a part of an annual charity beer festival at the Bottle Inn.

Nettle-eaters from as far as New York, Australia, Northern Ireland and Belgium have come to munch their way through specially provided 2ft stalks of nettles.

Rules demand that competitors must not use mouth-numbing substances. Beer-swigging, of course, is encouraged, especially as the taste of nettles has been described as 'a mixture of spinach and cow-pat.'

At the moment of writing the winning record is 26 yards of stinging nettles (23.77m).

Would-be nettle-eaters should know that Dorset's county motto is 'Who's Afear'd'!

8

SMUGGLING &
THE JURASSIC COAST

Today, when people speak of the Dorset coast they usually refer to the Jurassic Coast, a World Heritage Site, where remains of dinosaurs and fossils are constantly being found. In previous generations, however, any mention of the Dorset coast would instantly bring smugglers to mind – for Dorset, as nowhere else in the country, was the home of hundreds of these rogues, busily outwitting the law. It was a way of life and no one thought it at all wrong to evade those interfering customs officials.

When George III came annually to Weymouth on holiday the 'beneficial' effect on smuggling was remarkable – it stimulated the trade enormously! The fact is that the court officials, lords and ladies in the royal entourage, and the huge number of servants, grooms, cooks, etc. wanted and needed the smuggled goods – tea, wine, finery of all sorts. To a large extent the authorities turned a blind eye to the source of all the goods they expected to enjoy in Weymouth.

ISAAC GULLIVER – 'KING OF SMUGGLERS', THE GENTLE SMUGGLER WHO NEVER KILLED A MAN

It would take a very large volume to give a full account of the life of Isaac Gulliver (1745–1822). He was, without exaggeration, by far the most active and successful smuggler in Dorset. He amassed huge riches, owning no fewer than fifteen ships to ply his 'trade'. He bought himself many farms and built several large and splendid purpose-built houses in Dorset (purpose-built because they were filled with hiding-places for his smuggled goods). He never got caught, and ended his extraordinary life in great esteem and prosperity.

He made smuggling into big business, engaging over fifty helpers and keeping them constantly employed along the coast. With colossal impudence he actually dressed them in a kind of uniform or livery, with smock frocks and powdered hair – from which they gained the nickname of 'White-Wigs'.

Gulliver and his army of smugglers imported huge quantities of contraband goods – brandy, gin, tea, tobacco, sugar, lace and silks – into the creeks and inlets near what is now Bournemouth and Poole, but which was then mostly a completely desolate area. And beyond there, his smuggling activities along the south coast stretched widely from the Solent in Hampshire in the east, to Torbay in Devon. He even bought a farm at Eggardon Hill, one of Dorset's highest points, and created a plantation of trees to serve as a landmark for his smuggling ships.

Once, when he was told that the Excise men were coming to arrest him, Isaac Gulliver famously pretended to be a corpse, powdering his face to a deathly white and lying inert in a coffin. When the Revenue officers burst into his home they found his family grouped round his body, in deep mourning. Completely fooled, the Customs men departed, leaving the family to their gleeful 'grief'. To complete the deception, the local vicar solemnly (and it must be added, probably unwittingly) buried the coffin shortly afterwards . . . filled with stones!

Gulliver may even have benefited by some form of protection of George III himself, having warned the king of a French attempt to assassinate him. 'Let Gulliver smuggle as much as he like,' the grateful King is supposed to have said. However, Gulliver did avail himself of a proclamation pardoning smugglers if they joined the navy or found someone else to join up. From 1782 onwards he retired from his activities and became a respected citizen, wine-merchant, gentleman and banker, living in West Borough, Wimborne.

Isaac Gulliver's final years were a model of propriety – he even became a church warden at Wimborne Minster, where he is buried.

Former 'White-Wigs' were at his funeral, but his earlier activities were tactfully passed over. His memorial on the north wall of the West Tower is simply marked: 'Isaac Gulliver Esquire'.

Gulliver's pistol is to be seen in the Russell-Cotes Museum in Bournemouth – but his proud boast was that he had never used it to kill a man. He was far too clever, and, though a big and burly man, far too gentle.

One of Gulliver's many homes was West Howe Lodge at Kinson, now a part of Bournemouth. Sadly, this house was demolished in 1958 – and only then was it found to be riddled with secret doors, passages and hidden recesses. One door to a hiding-place was 10ft up a chimney!

There is an area in Poole called Lilliput – a none-too-subtle allusion to the fact that this was an area where Isaac Gulliver was frequently at work – in fact he owned Flag Farm here. It has no connection with Jonathan Swift, as some might suppose. Originally this area was called The Saltings, after the trade that was carried on there, but the name changed sometime in the nineteenth century as it was being developed.

THE OLD GEORGE INN, CHRISTCHURCH

The Old George Inn, in the centre of Christchurch, just a short distance from the priory, is just one of very many pubs in Dorset and neighbouring counties to have been made use of by smugglers – who were so numerous that it was a boast that 500 men could be brought together almost instantly whenever a cargo-boat was being unloaded. The goods would disappear to clandestine destinations just as quickly.

Rumour has it that beneath the Old George there are tunnels leading to the priory, where, so it is said, signalling lights were lit at the windows of St Michael's Loft (now a museum) to guide and warn the smuggling fraternity of any impending danger.

The Old George still possesses a collection of smugglers' memorabilia, including special casks which could be weighted down and sunk out of sight if ever a Revenue cutter stopped to search a suspected smuggler's vessel.

WOMEN'S SKIRTS AND 'FREQUENT PREGNANCIES'

Dorset's women helped their smuggling menfolk in many ways, especially as they could conceal flasks and bottles of brandy in their voluminous skirts and carry them from their coastal cottages to the various hiding-places further inland. Also, one excise man was heard to remark how very frequently the women seemed to get pregnant in those parts! However, these bulges were not always what they seemed. A story is told how customs men searched a cottage high and low for kegs of brandy, not realising that the women, feeding their babies, were sitting on them – with their skirts carefully draped around.

THE BATTLE OF MUDEFORD

In 1784 there was a pitched battle on Haven Quay at Mudeford near Christchurch between Customs men and the local 'gentlemen of the night'. A smuggler named William Parrott is believed to have fired the first shot which killed the commander of a sloop-of-war, HMS *Orestes,* as he stepped ashore to arrest a group busy unloading an illegal cargo of brandy and tea. This was the start of a fifteen-hour long battle, with the smugglers holed up in the Haven Inn.

As a result of this encounter one of the smugglers, George Coombes, was convicted and hanged at Newgate Gaol. His rotting body was brought back to Mudeford to hang in an iron cage at Haven Quay, as a warning to his smuggler friends.

IS YOUR NAME HERE?
ARE YOU A DESCENDANT OF A SMUGGLER?

So many men took part in smuggling activities and their descendants are almost certainly still living in this area, in and around Christchurch. Just for the record, here are just a few of the most notorious smugglers of yesteryear:

David BARRY
David BELL

George BOND
David BULL

William BURDEN
William CATON
William CHAPPLE
George COOMBES (hanged)
John COOPER
Peter DAVIS
Amos DOWDING
Jonathan EDWARDS
John GROVES
William HARDING
William HARRIS
George HUGHAM
William KENT
William MAY

John PARDY
William PARROTT
Jacob PENN
Jan PIERCE
Richard ROGERS
Joseph SAVON
Joseph SEVEN
Henry TROSS
Robert TAYLOR
Bone TUCKER
Henry VOSS
William WEBB
Henry WHITE
William WIBBAL and . . .

. . . John STREETER – who was probably the most famous and successful of all the Christchurch smugglers. He had a snuff factory just outside Christchurch, obviously being stocked with illegally imported tobacco. He was buried in the priory churchyard in 1824 at the age of seventy-four.

SMUGGLERS' HIDING PLACES

It was, of course, necessary to find useful places to store smuggled goods, if only temporarily – houses, farms, pubs, churches, specially made holes in remote country areas, ponds and pools where casks could be dropped out of sight were all used. Here are just a few of the many places known to have been utilised in this way:

Chesil Beach is unique – a long, straight, narrow bank of shingle stretching almost 17 miles from Burton Bradstock to Portland. Usefully for smugglers, there is the Fleet, a long lagoon lying alongside, between the mainland and Chesil Beach itself – providing relatively calm waters which are perfect for sinking barrels and casks ready for later collection. Smugglers who knew Chesil Beach well could easily judge their position along its length by the size of the pebbles – which vary from small pea-shingle at the Burton Bradstock end, to larger potato-sized stones at Portland.

St Andrew's Church, Kinson, is now in a suburb of Bournemouth, but it was the village church of a tiny village surrounded by heathland in Isaac Gulliver's day – and conveniently for his purposes, he lived nearby. The tower of St Andrew's was often used for storing smuggled goods, and even today we can see where ropes scored marks on the soft sandstone parapets as kegs of liquor were being hauled up and lowered down.

Near the church porch is a large chest tomb, with a pivoted side. It looks innocent enough, but it was easy for smugglers to open it up and put barrels and boxes inside, ready to be taken elsewhere when needed. Also in the churchyard at Kinson is a pathetic little memorial to one of the Kinson smugglers, Robert Trotman, 'barbarously Murder'd by the Revenue' in 1765:

> A little Tea one leaf I did not steal.
> For Guiltless Blood shed, I to God appeal.
> Put Tea in one scale, human Blood in t'other
> And think what 'tis to slay thy harmless Brother.

The Black Dog, Weymouth, was one of many local pubs involved in the smuggling business, and was the scene of a violent murder in the eighteenth century, when a Revenue Officer was killed while trying to arrest a smuggler.

Hardy's Cottage – the birthplace of Thomas Hardy – had been built by Hardy's great-grandfather in 1801, and for the first years of its isolated existence it was used as a smugglers' store, where up to eighty barrels of brandy were hidden. This was, of course, before Hardy was born, but in his notebook he recorded that the cottage still had an old bucket made out of one of these barrels.

Chideock. Smugglers landed goods between Charmouth and Seatown, and, like Isaac Gulliver, planted trees on the hilltops to serve as markers. Copses of trees grew at Charmouth, Seatown, Eype's Mouth and Stanton St Gabriel. The miller at Chideock itself had his special hiding place for tubs of spirits under the floor of his living-room at the mill.

Mother Siller's Channel is an inlet in Stanpit Marsh, Christchurch. It was much used by smugglers, who would bring their contraband goods ashore and hide them in a nearby pub – The Ship in Distress – kept by Hanna Siller. She obviously provided a wonderfully useful service to the smuggling community, who referred to her as

'The Angel of the Marsh'. The pub is still there and is well worth a visit.

Abbotsbury has its famous great tithe barn – the largest in England – built by the Benedictine monks in the 1390s. Smugglers in Abbotsbury had their headquarters at a pub now called The Ilchester Arms – though it was formerly known as The Ship Inn. In this twenty-first century, the great tithe barn has been turned into a children's fun area where they can learn about smuggling, and meet Isaac Gulliver in a continuous DVD presentation.

Langton Matravers has had a number of churches, but the main part of one which was built in the early nineteenth century had to be pulled down and rebuilt, probably because of the weakening effects of heavy barrels of wine and spirits which were once stored in the space between the dome-like ceiling of the church and the upper tiled roof. Only the tower was kept and incorporated in the present building, completed and opened in 1876.

HELPING GRANDAD

A fascinating fragment of a young boy's diary has survived, giving an account of how, aged ten, he was used as a look-out by his grandfather, Charles Hayward, as contraband was loaded into the old church roof. The boy's name was Charlie Dean and at the beginning of his diary he writes:

> I was born the 28th day of June A.D. 1859, being the anniversary of Queen Victoria's coronation day, in Langton Matravers

The story he tells is clearly dated 23 October 1869, so he must have been just over ten when the events he describes took place. Smuggling, by its very nature, was a secret activity, so the following account is probably unique:

> Today happened great adventures with Grandfather. Last evening he asked me if I felt well enough to assist him in some business matter. I replied that . . . I was at his service. This evening, just after dusk, I was requested by my Grandfather to stand outside the Church gate – but not to look too

involved with anything particular, and so I must needs walk to and fro past the gate, and <u>not</u> stand too still. I found this nothing but necessary, since there was a cold wind. My Grandfather also gave me strict instructions to alert him – he being within the Church – if a Peeler-Policeman came up or down the road.

Seven gentlemen arrived variously to meet my Grandfather, and they all went inside the Church. A Peeler came down from Garfield, past me, and thence on to Stepps. I had given the alert (taking my cap off, shaking it, and putting it on again) and whilst the Peeler walked bye all was silent in the Church, nor any light.

Presently came two stone carts from Garfield end, and the seven gentlemen came out and assisted the drivers with unloading the stones; these were stacked flat down and not up-down. The men then brought in barrels of all sizes and different shapes. All together this went into the Church – I could not see where, but I heard a bell make a half-sounding, and heard a man say something bad. They then I think came to the porch, and the two drivers took papers from my Grandfather, and re-loaded the stone and drove off to Stepps. I heard much talking; my Grandfather came out, thanked me profusely for my assistance, and gave me a gold coin. I went home, and straight to bed.

Charles Hayward, of Langton Matravers (born in 1796) was the grandfather in the story told above. He led an interesting and varied life and was a successful businessman working in the quarrying trade. He was also Langton's first sub-postmaster, and the village's highly respected churchwarden and parish clerk. He died in 1879, aged eighty-two, taking his secrets with him to the grave. Only when his grandson's diary came to light did his friends and family know the truth about his smuggling activities!

A DORSET SMUGGLER'S SONG

If you wake at midnight, and hear a horse's feet
Don't go drawing back the blind, or looking in the street.
Them as asks no questions, isn't told a lie.
Watch the wall, my darling, while the Gentlemen go by.

Five and twenty ponies
Trotting though the dark,
Brandy for the Parson,
'Baccy for the Clerk.
Laces for a lady, letters for a spy,
And watch the wall, my darling, while the Gentlemen go by.

THE JURASSIC COAST WORLD HERITAGE SITE

The cliffs that make up the Dorset and Devon coast are an important site for fossils and provide a continuous record of life on land and in the sea since 185 million years ago. Here are some of the basic facts:

The site stretches from Orcombe Point near Exmouth in East Devon to Old Harry Rocks near Swanage in East Dorset.

The length of the Jurassic Coast is 95 miles.

It was given its World Heritage Site status in 2001.

The Jurassic Coast was the second wholly-natural World Heritage Site to be designated in the United Kingdom (the first site was the Giant's Causeway and Causeway Coast in County Antrim, Northern Ireland).

It's possible to walk the entire length of the Jurassic Coast, using the South West Coast Path.

The Jurassic Coast consists of Triassic, Jurassic and Cretaceous cliffs, spanning the Mesozoic Era, documenting 185 million years of geological history.

The highest point on the Jurassic Coast, and on the entire south coast of Britain, is Golden Cap, at 627ft.

In a 2005 poll of *Radio Times* readers, the Jurassic Coast was named as the fifth greatest natural wonder in Britain.

Huge quantities of fossils and bones of many kinds of dinosaurs can easily be found on Dorset shores – and the constant erosion of the cliffs continually exposes yet more and more. It is a geologist's heaven.

The Dorset coast has now been officially confirmed as a future offshore wind farm. Construction is set to begin in 2016, and potentially the windmills there will produce 0.9 gigawatts of energy. They will be seen out to sea beyond Old Harry Rocks.

WHY 'JURASSIC'?

The word 'Jurassic' has become much used and prominent partly because of the film *Jurassic Park*, and also because of the popular term 'Jurassic Coast', used to refer to the Dorset and East Devon UNESCO World Heritage Site. However, in fact, this site consists of geological remains of four periods: Triassic (250–205 million years ago), Jurassic (205–135 million years ago), Cretaceous (135–65 million years ago), and Tertiary (65–1.6 million years ago).

The words are familiar, but somewhat artificially invented. 'Triassic' simply means that it is one of the 'three' periods in the 'Mesozoic' era. 'Cretaceous' means that it is characterised by 'chalk' deposits. But what about 'Jurassic'? It's not often realised that this word is derived from the Jura – the mountain range in eastern France, where the rocks date from the 'Jurassic' period. And the word 'Jura' itself comes from a Celtic root meaning 'forest'. It was originally simply the name for a mountain forest – so Dorset's 'Jurassic' coast has an odd word-history.

MARY ANNING (1799–1847) FOSSIL-COLLECTOR AND SELF-TAUGHT PALAEONTOLOGIST

The science of palaeontology was virtually brought into being by a twelve-year-old Lyme Regis girl, Mary Anning, when she discovered the first ichthyosaur in 1811. Mary was lucky to have been born in Lyme Regis, where cliff-falls are constantly revealing huge deposits of fossils. Her father, a poor cabinet-maker, eked out his income by finding and selling curious shells and fossils, so it was only natural that his little daughter ran about the seashore looking for things to help him. Such fossils were collectors' items in the early nineteenth century, though they were little understood.

Sadly, Mary's father died when she was only eleven, and so she and her fourteen-year-old brother were forced to step up their fossil-collecting to earn desperately needed money. They set up a table near a local inn to sell their discoveries to the tourists who were beginning to enjoy the seaside (it was the time of Jane Austen's *Persuasion* and Louisa Musgrove's famous fall).

Before he died, Mary's father had taught her to use a hammer and chisel to knock interesting things out of the cliff-face, or break up rocks on the sea-shore, and she became expert in sensing where she could expect to find good specimens. Her lucky break came in 1811, when she was only twelve, and she discovered the very first ichthyosaur – which is now in London's Natural History Museum. Later, in 1821, she discovered the first two plesiosaur skeletons ever found, and then in 1828 the first pterodactyl skeleton located outside of Germany. It was an astonishing achievement for a young girl who in many respects was hardly educated. As an enterprising teenager she opened a shop at Lyme and bit by bit she taught herself more and more about her finds until she became in effect one of the world's leading experts in palaeontology.

Her energy and self-taught skill and knowledge led to her becoming consulted and admired by the scientific community. Frustratingly for her, however, many of the great scientists of the day took her discoveries and her insights as their own, without acknowledging the debt they owed to her. After all, she was poor, uneducated, of very low social standing, and – worst of all – only a woman!

Her reputation and true status have become appreciated only gradually over time. She was one of Dorset's most remarkable women. Tragically, she was only forty-seven when she died of breast cancer. She is buried in the church at Lyme.

NEW WORDS FOR OLD BONES

New discoveries demanded to be named, so following the findings of Mary Anning and the increasing number of other fossil-collectors, scientists needed to classify them. Weird new names were invented – and these were almost as fascinating as the creatures themselves. Here are just a few – connected with Mary Anning's Dorset discoveries. . . .

Ammonites are among the most easily found fossils. They are strange, flat spiral shells with all kinds of bumps and ridges. Some are very small, others can be a metre or more and too heavy to carry. Looking like curled-up serpents, they were earlier called 'Snake stones'. But the name 'ammonite', which was finally given to them, is curiously derived – from the ancient Egyptian ram-headed god, Ammon.

Belemnites are fossils pointed like a dart. Before they gained their scientific name they were known as 'thunderbolts' or 'thunder-stones' or 'elf-bolts'. The name 'belemnite' is derived from the Greek word, belemnon, a dart.

Dinosaur – 'terrible lizard'. The word was first coined by Sir Richard Owen in 1841 from the two Greek words deinos, meaning terrible, and sauros, a lizard.

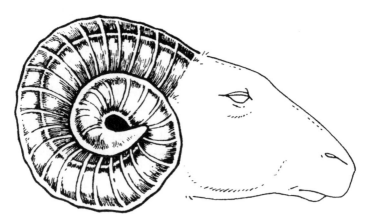

Ammon, the Egyptian ram-headed god whose name is used for the 'ammonite' fossils.

Durdle Door. The name of this famous landmark on the Jurassic Coast probably means 'hill with a hole in it'.

Ichthyosaur – the first of which was found by Mary Anning at Lyme Regis. Its name is derived from the Greek word for a fish – ichthys. Therefore it is a 'fish-lizard'.

Plesiosaur – when first discovered, it was a complete mystery. The puzzled scientists described it as 'a snake threaded through the body of a turtle'. In 1821 a name was proposed which simply meant 'it looks like a lizard' – from the Greek plesios, near, and sauros, lizard. Even the man who invented the word, W.D. Conybeare, admitted that the word 'may appear rather vague'. Nevertheless it was a word which has stuck!

Pterodactyl is the popular name for the **pterosauria** or 'winged lizards'. When Mary Anning found the first English specimen in 1828, there had been other similar discoveries abroad, but no one knew what they were – even thinking that they were sea-going creatures. When it was realised that the wings were for flying, the name 'Ornithosaur' (bird-lizard) was suggested – but it was the German Johann Kaup who gave them the name 'Pterosaur' in 1834 – six years after Mary Anning's discovery. The popular name 'Pterodactyl' was coined by the French scientist Georges Cuvier in 1809 – meaning 'finger-wing.'

AND THE BIGGEST DORSET MONSTER
STILL WAITING TO BE DUG UP?

In October 2009 news broke that probably the biggest prehistoric monster ever discovered anywhere on earth is lying, waiting to be dug out of the Dorset cliffs where it has been hidden for the past 150 million years.

It has been identified as a pliosaur – a type of Plesiosaur, the group of giant aquatic dinosaurs which swam in the oceans feeding on ichthyosaurs and fellow plesiosaurs.

So far, only the fossilised skull and jawbone of this pliosaur has been unearthed and just this enormous section is 8ft long. From this measurement, it is calculated that the creature probably had a colossal overall length of 52ft!

The exact location of this find is being kept secret, to keep unwanted diggers away, but Dr Richard Edmonds, Dorset County Council's earth science manager for the Jurassic Coast, has said: 'The ground is dipping very steeply, and it is such a huge specimen it will be buried beneath layer upon layer of rock, so we will have to wait patiently for the next big landslide.'

Dorset County Museum, eventually, will house this monster. Sooner or later it will be fully unearthed, perhaps in five years' time – or fifty? Who knows? Maybe our grandchildren will gawp at it in wonder.

9

CASTLES &
CURIOUS STONES

Dorset has scores of castles. Of course, it depends how you define a castle – for the name 'castle' is also applied to several ancient earthworks such as Maiden Castle. The county is also strewn with hundreds of mysterious standing stones, whose purposes defy imagination.

Bow and Arrow Castle, also known as Rufus Castle, a curious and picturesque ruin at Church Ope Cove.

PART ONE – CASTLES

The author of *Castles of Dorset*, Phil Wilton, identified no fewer than seventy-two castles in the county, and listed them in eight categories:

Castles still in existence (8)
Avon Castle, Brownsea Castle, Durlston Castle, Pennsylvania Castle, Portland Castle, Sherborne New Castle, Woodsford Castle, Wyke Castle.

Castles in ruins (9)
Bow and Arrow Castle, Christchurch Castle, Corfe Castle, Highcliffe Castle (now restored), Lulworth Castle (now restored), Marshwood Castle, Sandsfoot Castle, Sherborne Old Castle, Sturminster Newton Castle.

Hill forts (11) (i.e. ancient earthworks with no buildings)
Abbotsbury Castle, Badbury Rings, Cattistock Castle, Coney's Castle, Crawford Castle, Dudsbury Castle, Duntish Castle, Eggardon Castle, Lambert's Castle, Maiden Castle, Weatherby Castle.

Possible castles (18)
Bere Regis Castle, Bindon Castle, Blacknor Castle, Bridport Castle, Burton Bradstock Castle, Cerne Castle, Leigh Castle, Mohun Castle, Nettlecombe Castle, Pillesdoen Castle, Poole Castle, Puddletown Castle, Selfridge's Castle, Stephen's Castle, Storborough Castle, Stourpaine Castle, Stourton Caundel Castle, Wimborne Castle.

Buildings (4)
Castle Bunter, Cranbourne Castle, Rats Castle, Wolfeton Castle.

Ramparts only (8)
Chideock Castle, Corfe Castle – The Rings, Cranborne Castle Hill, East Chelborough Castle Hill, East Chelborough Stake Farm, Gillingham Castle, Powerstock Castle, Shaftesbury Castle.

Vanished Castles (4)
Dorchester Castle, Parkstone Castle, Strangways Castle, Studland Castle, Wareham Castle.

Castles known by another name (8)
(Truth to tell, some of these may never have existed, or are probably simply misspellings – e.g. 'Conig's' may well be 'Coney's)
Abbotsbury Castle, Branksea Castle, Chidrick Castle, Conig's Castle (Hill fort), Drummer's Castle, Piddlewood Castle, Rufus Castle, Twineham Castle, Weymouth Castle.

Here are some of some of Dorset's most important castles, which no visitor should miss, beginning with the most iconic of all: Corfe Castle.

CORFE CASTLE, WHERE KING JOHN STARVED HIS PRISONERS TO DEATH

It is odd to think that £700,000 was spent in 2006 to preserve the ruins of Corfe Castle – but it was disputed that it was arguably Britain's most romantic ruin! Certainly its jagged silhouette, high on a hill, is a spectacular sight, and today it is one of the National Trust's most popular tourist attractions, especially for children, who love to run around the ruins and peer out of its arrow-slits.

People always remember the murder of King Edward the Martyr and the Cromwellian siege, when Lady Bankes defied the Parliamentarians for months. But the centuries in between are often less remembered. For example, in the civil war between King Stephen and his cousin Matilda in the twelfth century, Matilda held Corfe against the king's armies.

It was King John (reigned 1199–1216), of Magna Carta fame, who most enjoyed Corfe Castle, using it as a royal residence and keeping his crown and his treasure here. He added greatly to the building, and found it an extremely useful dumping-ground for his enemies. He flung them into the dungeons and simply let them starve to death. After murdering his nephew Arthur, who had a better claim to the throne than he had, he forced Arthur's sister, Eleanor, the 'Damsel of Britanny', to live under house arrest at Corfe. She was later removed to Bristol, enduring forty years of imprisonment.

Another royal prisoner here was Edward II, after he had been deposed. He spent some time in Corfe before being hustled off to Berkeley Castle in Gloucestershire to be cruelly murdered.

Corfe was owned by all successive monarchs until Queen Elizabeth I gave it to her court favourite, Sir Christopher Hatton, who later became Lord Chancellor. It was then sold to Sir John Bankes and was owned by the Bankes family until 1982, when they bequeathed it to the National Trust.

HIGHCLIFFE CASTLE, 'HOW NICE IT IS TO SEE SOMEONE ELSE IN DIFFICULTIES AT SEA!'

One of Dorset's most curious and attractive castles is Highcliffe Castle, to the east of Christchurch. It was built between 1830 and 1835 for the grandson of John Stuart, 3rd Earl of Bute, who was George III's Prime Minister in 1762–3. The castle has had a chequered history. In its heyday as a country house, it was visited by royalty and many notables, including:

Queen Marie Amelie, wife of King Louis-Philippe of France
Queen Sophia Matilda of the Netherlands
Crown Prince Gustav of Sweden (later King Gustav V)
The Prince and Princess of Wales (later King Edward VII and Queen Alexandra)
Mr and Mrs William Gladstone
The German Emperor Wilhelm II (the Kaiser) – who paid for some redecoration and gave a stained-glass window (sadly now lost) featuring the German Eagle
Dame Nellie Melba, who sang there to entertain the other guests

Having been sold and used successively as a children's convalescent home, a Roman Catholic seminary, and suffering two major fires, it is now enjoying a new lease of life as a popular tourist attraction. Owned by Christchurch Borough Council and restored with the help of the Heritage Lottery Fund, it hosts a constant succession of exhibitions and concerts and has become a popular venue for weddings.

It's a strange history for a strange castle – and perhaps strangest of all is its architecture, for it is constructed from bits and pieces from disused French abbeys, so that it looks (and is) much older than the date when it was built. And among this odd but attractive conglomeration of architectural fragments are what at first appear to be battlements, but on closer inspection turn out to be a famous Latin quotation from Lucretius (*c.* 99–55 BC), carved out in letters of stone along the parapet between the two main parts of the building, reading:

SUAVE, MARI MAGNO TURBANTIBUS AEQUORA
VENTIS
E TERRA MAGNUM ALTERIUS SPECTARE LABOREM

'How nice it is to see someone else struggling in difficulties at sea when you are safe on land yourself!' What a cruel quotation to carve on a beautiful castle! It is pure *schadenfreude* – as perhaps the Kaiser might have said. Well, he did help to pay for it.

LULWORTH CASTLE, FORMER HOME OF GEORGE IV'S SECRET WIFE

Nowadays, since 1998, Lulworth Castle is one of the most beautiful visitor attractions in Dorset, with the animal farm, picnic areas, children's playground, stable café, shop, and of course the beautiful castle itself. It is a triumph of enterprise, rescuing a lovely family home which was gutted by fire in the 1920s to transform itself, phoenix-like, into a vibrant new existence.

From the exterior it is almost a child's vision of what a castle should look like: massive, foursquare, with large round towers at each corner. It was never a military castle, but was originally built in the early seventeenth century as a hunting lodge by Thomas Howard. It was bought by Humphrey Weld in 1641 and since then, to this day, Lulworth Castle has been owned by successive generations of the Weld family, descendants of Sir Humphrey Weld (1546–1610) a wealthy merchant who had been Lord Mayor of London.

Importantly, the Weld family have always been staunch Catholics, and near the castle is the beautiful St Mary's Chapel, built in

1786–7 – the first free-standing Roman Catholic chapel to be built in England since the Reformation (see page 51).

Tragically, one of the Weld owners of Lulworth Castle, Edward Weld (1741–75), was killed in a riding accident shortly after marrying a ravishingly beautiful seventeen-year-old by the name of Mary-Anne Smythe. As a young widow, Mary then married Thomas Fitzherbert, thus acquiring a name which was to become famous in English royal history – Maria Fitzherbert (as she liked to be called).

Widowed a second time, she entered London society and quickly attracted the attention of 'Prinny' – the Prince Regent – who was later to become King George IV. He fell desperately in love with her, and pleaded with her to marry him. They both knew this was impossible, because Maria was a Catholic, and it was (and still is) illegal for an English monarch to marry a Catholic. Nevertheless, Prinny threatened suicide if she did not accept him. So, in very great secrecy, they married.

Their marriage was an open secret, but no one dared mention it, even when Prinny married again, this time bigamously, to his cousin Caroline of Brunswick, whom he hated. Later, George and Maria drifted apart, but when he lay dying, George IV asked to be buried 'with whatever ornaments might be upon my person at the time of death.'

It was the Duke of Wellington who noted that on his deathbed George was wearing a black ribbon round his neck carrying a small locket. That locket is still with George's remains in Windsor's vault. It contains a miniature portrait of the only woman the king ever really loved – Mrs Fitzherbert, formerly Mrs Edward Weld, of Lulworth Castle.

As for Maria, she was buried wearing three rings – one from each of her husbands.

SHERBORNE'S 'OLD CASTLE', A JEWEL FOR THE QUEEN DOES THE TRICK

There are in fact *two* Sherborne Castles: the 'old' and the 'new' – both having links with Sir Walter Raleigh. In 1592, when Sir Walter first caught sight of the 'old' Sherborne Castle, he was instantly overcome with a passionate desire to own it for himself. He happened to be riding down from London to Plymouth when he glanced down into the valley. He was entranced by what he saw – an ancient twelfth-century castle, originally built by Roger de Caen, Bishop of Salisbury, then the most powerful man in England after the king.

The story goes that Raleigh made an impetuous gesture of delight which made his horse stumble and throw him in the mud, but Sir Walter wasn't in the least troubled – he was too preoccupied with the sight of the castle. At that time Raleigh was a court favourite of Elizabeth I – indeed there was a strong physical attraction between the two. Shrewd as ever, Raleigh knew how to exploit his close relationship with the queen, and gave her a jewel worth two hundred and fifty pounds – with the tacit understanding that she would nudge the castle's occupant out and pave the way for him to take it over.

Queen Elizabeth agreed, and quickly ensured that Raleigh should own the castle. But then, horror of horrors, she made the awful discovery that Raleigh had been secretly married for some months to one of her ladies in waiting! For a courtier to marry without her permission was virtual treason – and she instantly imprisoned them both in the Tower of London.

After five weeks, Raleigh and his wife Bess were released from the Tower, but they were still banished from Elizabeth's sight forever. In the event, Raleigh's banishment lasted just five years, but in that time he had the leisure and opportunity to try to settle into his newly acquired Sherborne Castle.

However, he soon realised that it would take far more money and effort than he could afford. He therefore turned his attention to a Tudor hunting lodge, within sight of the old castle, and with new determination he devoted his energy to enlarging this into what then became Sherborne's 'New Castle'.

Sherborne's 'Old Castle' still remained habitable, but suffered during the Civil War. Naturally, it was a Royalist stronghold and was twice besieged by Parliamentarian forces. In 1645 it was 'sleighted' by General Fairfax – the somewhat euphemistic word for being blown up.

Today, the ruins of 'old' Sherborne Castle are tranquil and picturesque. Since 1984 they have been maintained by English Heritage, open to the public who enjoy wandering round, learning its history, and having picnics in its beautiful grounds.

SHERBORNE'S 'NEW' CASTLE', THE DIGBY OSTRICH, EATING A HORSESHOE

Sherborne's 'New Castle' is the lovely country house which was originally the hunting lodge developed by Sir Walter Raleigh. Even before Raleigh was beheaded in 1618, the estate was forfeited to the crown and in 1617 King James I sold it to Sir John Digby, 1st Earl of Bristol. From that date until now, the Digby family has owned it, lived in it, developed it and brought countless treasures to it. Sherborne New Castle is now one of the most fascinating great houses in Britain. Owned privately, it is open to visitors throughout the summer months.

Inside the house visitors may see magnificent furniture, porcelain, stunning decoration, and a wonderful collection of portraits. Outside, in the grounds landscaped by 'Capability' Brown – who contrived the 20-hectare lake and a cascading waterfall – are Sir Walter Raleigh's superb Virginia cedar trees, a rare Japanese ghinko tree, and 'Raleigh's Seat'. Here, according to the well-known tradition, Raleigh was sitting and enjoying smoking his pipe when a well-meaning servant drenched him with a bucket of water – thinking that his master was on fire!

And the ostrich?
Throughout the castle the 'Digby Ostrich' is to be found – a strange heraldic bird with which the Digby family has been associated for at least six hundred years. It forms the crest on the Digby coat of arms and makes its somewhat eccentric appearance on a pair of andirons in the Green Drawing Room.

The Digby Ostrich with a horse shoe in its beak.

According to an odd medieval belief, ostriches had extraordinary digestive powers and ate any piece of iron they could find. In heraldry, ostriches always have a piece of iron in their beaks. The proud Digby Ostrich has a horseshoe.

Traditionally, the Digby Ostrich holds the horseshoe upside down – the 'unlucky' way, as this lets the good luck fall out of it. But this is deliberate, because the Digby family motto is DEO NON FORTUNA, meaning that they trust in God and not in luck. Symbolically, the ostrich signifies watchfulness and strength.

THREE CASTLES ON PORTLAND BILL

Portland Bill is only 4½ miles long and 1¾ wide. Nevertheless, three castles are built there – each very different from the other two.

Bow and Arrow Castle – sometimes called Rufus Castle – is the oldest of the three, and may be the keep of a castle built during the reign of William Rufus (1087–1100), son of the Conqueror. It is near the Portland Museum, along Church Ope Road, and is totally in ruins. The walls are 7ft thick, built, naturally, of Portland stone. It is possibly a fifteenth-century replacement of an earlier castle.

Recently, Bow and Arrow Castle was sold for £1, in the hope that the new owner would stabilise it. Little, if anything, has been done.

Portland Castle, by contrast, is firmly dated, to have been completed in 1540, during the reign of Henry VIII. It is the most complete castle in Dorset, seen today virtually as it was when it was built, for defence against pirates and the 'wicked' French. It was used for defence even during the Second World War, but now it is happily open for tourists.

Pennsylvania Castle is interestingly named because it was built in the last three years of the eighteenth century by John Penn, the grandson of William Penn, the founder of Pennsylvania. It was designed by James Wyatt, the fashionable architect of that time. King George III himself visited the site on one of his holiday visits to Weymouth and granted the land to John Penn. In fact, one of the king's daughters came to open it when it was completed. It has been a hotel for part of its history, but now it is once again a private house – still, however, visible from various locations.

'John Penn's Bath' is a curious construction. The castle itself is high above sea level, so Penn ordered a huge 'bath' to be made in the cliff-side, half-way down to the beach. His servants would be required to lug buckets of water up from the sea to fill it. The Portlanders, however, complained that he had built this 'bath' on common land and so would be required to pay for the use of it! In disgust, John Penn abandoned the scheme – but the 'bath' is still to be found, but only by those who relish climbing through brambles down a steep cliff.

PART TWO – CURIOUS STONES
CLAVELL TOWER

Surely no 'folly' has been given such a generous and unusual facelift as Clavell Tower – the famous landmark on a cliff-top overlooking Kimmeridge Bay. It probably holds the record for having been removed, stone by stone (16,272 of them) and then rebuilt 82ft away from its former site to be refurbished as a self-catering holiday apartment with electricity, water, a kitchen and a bathroom.

The history of this curious folly is that it was built in 1830 by a wealthy clergyman, the Revd John Richards Clavell, partly as an observation tower and partly just for fun on a dramatic part of the coastline. It became used as a coastguard station and Thomas Hardy loved it, visiting it, so it is said, with one of his early loves, Eliza Nicholls, who was a daughter of a coastguard official working in Kimmeridge. With another literary connection, it inspired P.D. James, who based her novel *The Black Tower* on it.

Ultimately, Clavell Tower became derelict and seemed certain to fall into the sea as a result of coastal erosion, but thanks to public support and with funding from the Heritage Lottery Fund, the whole four-storey tower was carefully dismantled in 2007 and re-erected further inland – with the last brick being put in place on 25 February 2008. Later that year it opened as a holiday apartment, and can now be hired as such from the Landmark Trust. The project took 18 months, and cost £898,000.

CHARBOROUGH PARK GOTHIC TOWER

Frustratingly for the general public, the Gothic Tower in Charborough Park is seldom to be seen, as the park is opened only or rare occasions. However, it is, according to a National Trust Guide, 'one of the finest folly-towers in Britain'. It is an octagonal five-storey tower rising to a height of 120ft. A plaque on the ground on the ground floor explains:

> This tower was built by Edward Drax, Esquire, in the year 1790, during the short time he was the possessor of Charborough. It was struck by lightning on the 29th of November 1838, which so damaged it that it became necessary to take down the greater part. It was rebuilt in 1839 by John Samuel Wanley Sawbridge Erle Drax Esquire who carried it forty feet higher than it was originally built making the present height upwards of one hundred feet.

This lengthily-named John Samuel Wanley Sawbridge Erle Drax radically changed the course of the main Dorchester–Wimborne road in order to preserve his privacy, moving a turnpike further away from his house and making the road travel in a huge semi-circle around his estate. He then surrounded his property with one of the longest brick walls in England, using more than two million bricks. A local man tried to sue Drax for the loss of the road, but his efforts were unsuccessful. Drax was triumphant, but unfortunately for him, his new turnpike lost money almost immediately because of the coming of the Wimborne–Dorchester railway.

The Tower, Charborough Park, setting for Thomas Hardy's novel, Two on a Tower.

Charborough Park Tower has been given lasting fame because this was the centrepiece of Thomas Hardy's novel, *Two on a Tower*, published in 1882, in which he sets 'two infinitesimal lives against the stupendous background of the stellar universe.' In this novel a young lady comes to the tower 'in a gleaming landau . . . [and] she had heard that from the summit four counties could be seen. Whatever pleasurable effect was to be derived from looking into four counties at the same time, she resolved to enjoy.'

And this is exactly the view provided by Charborough Park Tower.

THE CROSS-IN-HAND STONE

The Cross-in-Hand Stone, or 'Crossy Hand' as it is called locally, is a small round pillar, 3ft 6in tall. Thomas Hardy describes its location: 'On a lonely table-land above the Vale of Blackmore, between High-Stoy and Bubb-Down hills, and commanding in clear weather views that extend from the English to the Bristol Channel, stands a pillar, apparently mediaeval, called Cross-and-Hand or Christ-in-Hand.'

It has attracted several stories and legends about its origin, but the fact is, no one knows for sure how old it is or why it is there. One story tells that it marks the grave of a murderer who had sold his soul to the Devil. It may be a Roman marker or boundary stone – or perhaps placed here even earlier in Celtic times – or later during the Middle Ages. Who knows? It may have had a cross on it – but one feature that gives it its name is the faint figure of a woman with her hands crossed which can just still be discerned on it.

Thomas Hardy gave it additional fame by telling one of the legends in ballad form, 'The Lost Pyx'. In this, a medieval priest loses his pyx on the way to a dying man. He retraces his steps, only to find a strange light guiding him to the place where he had dropped it – and kneeling in a circle, adoring it, are wild animals – squirrels, rabbits, badgers, oxen, sheep, and 'many a member seldom seen of Nature's family.' In gratitude, the priest erects this stone on the place where he found his pyx. Hardy also makes use of this strange stone in *Tess of the D'Urbervilles*, when Tess places her hand on it, swearing never to tempt Alec D'Urberville.

An old gypsy woman once told a local historian that this was a wishing-stone, and that anyone placing a hand on it, and making a wish, would be sure to find that wish come true.

THE ANCIENT STONES OF DORSET

The Ancient Stones of Dorset is a compellingly fascinating book by Peter Knight, in which he discusses the huge number of standing stones and stone circles in the county. It is impossible to do justice to the wealth of mysterious Celtic stones in Dorset. Anyone wishing to follow up the details of the few stones mentioned here should get hold of this book.

These stones, linking up with long barrows, round barrows, chambered tombs, henges, ley mark stones, Roman stones and stone crosses, combine to form an astonishing number of mysterious ley lines. Peter Knight has spent a lifetime literally unearthing previously hidden or unnoticed ancient stones. Stone circles, dating back to the Neolithic and Bronze ages – roughly 3,000 to 1,000 BC – take us back to an ancient world we can hardly imagine. Dorset's most famous stone circles are at:

Nine Stones, 4 miles west of Dorchester, just past Winterbourne Abbas on the A35. It is perhaps the most famous Dorset stone circle, noted by John Aubrey in the seventeenth century, William Stukeley in the eighteenth, and given much attention by modern archaeologists, including Professor Alexander Thom, discoverer of the 'megalithic yard' (2.72ft / 82cm). This circle has been shown to lie at a meeting-point of three ley lines, one of which leads to Stonehenge itself.

Rempstone, beside the B3351 Studland to Corfe Castle road, on the left as you go towards Corfe. Here are nine stones in a semi-circle, obviously with the southern half of the circle now missing. This circle lies at the north end of a ley-line running south-west to Chalbury hill fort.

Hampton Hill Stone Circle, about half a mile north-west of Portesham, reached from the coast path, which passes close by. Peter Knight describes in detail how this circle possesses a subtle relationship to the Hellstone (see opposite) and how it is aligned to neighbouring hills and tumuli.

Kingston Russell Stone Circle, about 2 miles north of Abbotsbury. Eighteen ancient stones are positioned in a flattened circle, approximately 90ft x 80ft. They are now all prone, but at least one was still standing in the nineteenth century. The largest is about 8ft long. The circle has been shown to belong to a ley-line marked by a number of tumuli.

Littlemayne Stones (a former stone circle), about 2 miles south of Stinsford. One of the stones in this circle is known as 'The Giant without a Head'.

THE HELLSTONE

The Hellstone is a magnificent Neolithic dolmen consisting of nine gigantic upright stones ('orthostats') supporting an equally gigantic capstone, about half a mile north of Portesham. Sadly, it had collapsed by the mid-nineteenth century, but was reconstructed in 1866. Nevertheless, the stones and the site are original, and what we see today is arguably the most impressively atmospheric group of ancient stones in Dorset.

Legend has it that the Hellstone was thrown here from Portland by the Devil when he was playing quoits – a stone-throwing legend which is typical of ancient explanations of these mysterious dolmens.

The Hellstone has been shown to be on a ley-line leading to Maiden Castle and beyond.

THE DEVIL IN DORSET

The Agglestone – a huge natural rock formation near Studland, 80ft in circumference – carries the legend that the Devil, busy as ever, hurled it from the Needles, trying to hit Corfe Castle, or perhaps Bindon Abbey. The Agglestone has also been called the 'Devil's Anvil' or the 'Devil's Nightcap'. However, its very name, 'Agglestone', is derived from the Saxon word *helig* (modern German, *heilig*), meaning 'holy' – suggesting that it belongs to some sort of pagan sacred past.

Other 'Devil places' in Dorset include: the Devil's Armchair (standing stones at Corscombe), the Devil's Stone (on Black Hill above Bere Regis), and the Devil's Spoon and Trencher (earthworks at Iwerne Courtney).

'THE GREY MARE AND HER COLTS'

This intriguing name is given to a Scheduled Ancient Monument which has been called 'Dorset's best example of a megalithic chambered long barrow.' It is to be found about 1½ miles north-west of Portesham, and consists of a roughly triangular mound, rising to 4ft in height and measuring about 75ft long by 35ft at its widest. The chamber itself has collapsed, but measured about 7ft x 7ft. Two megaliths stand nearby, one more or less square and the other diamond-shaped. The site is complex and has been interestingly described by Peter Knight. Of crucial importance is the fact that the axis of this barrow is aligned to the Summer Solstice/Winter Solstice sunsets.

Dorset is crammed with prehistoric sites, standing stones, ley-lines and mysterious relics of the past. Even the names given to many of these stir memories of an ancient world we can hardly begin to understand. A lifetime study is needed.

THE HARDY MONUMENT

Seen for miles, the Hardy Monument stands at 776ft on the hills between Dorchester and Bridport. It was erected by public subscription in 1844 – when the writer Thomas Hardy, in nearby Bockhampton, was just four years old. The monument, of course, is in memory of Admiral Sir Thomas Masterman Hardy, Bart, CCB, Flag Captain to Lord Nelson on HMS *Victory* at the Battle of Trafalgar.

Thomas Hardy the writer always liked to think that he was in some way linked to Dorset's other memorable Hardy, and he was pleased to be able to see the Hardy Monument from his home at Max Gate.

The Hardy Monument, one of the highest places in Dorset.

Seeing the monument, we cannot help but think of both Hardys – the admiral and the writer. The landmark is unmissable – designed by Arthur Dyke Troyte – but has been constantly ridiculed and rubbished as unworthy of its purpose. Some rude comparisons include:

> 'a 70-foot sink plunger'
> 'a chess-piece'
> 'a peppermill'
> 'a candlestick telephone'
> 'a factory chimney with a crinoline'

Since 1900 the monument has belonged to the National Trust – and it was one of their earliest purchases.

10

MEN & WOMEN

Dorset has produced and has been the home of many extraordinary people. Some are famous, others less so – though they deserve to be remembered. Writers are dealt with in another chapter, but here are Dorset men and women who have made their mark in many and various ways.

THE TOLPUDDLE MARTYRS

Individually, they are hardly remembered by name, but together the six Dorset men who are known as the 'Tolpuddle Martyrs' are world famous and their story has made a huge impact on British history. To honour them, here are the 'Six Men of Dorset'.

GEORGE LOVELESS	1797–1874
JAMES LOVELESS	1798–1873
THOMAS STANFIELD	1790–1864
JOHN STANFIELD	1812–98
JAMES BRINE	1813–1902
JAMES HAMMETT	1811–92

Their story is straightforward and quickly told. Living as Dorset labourers in the 1830s, their wages of seven shillings a week were so meagre as to bring them and their families to starvation level. They begged for a rise, pointing out that Hampshire labourers were getting ten shillings per week – but the local squire and vicar sided with the farmers and against the labourers. So, when it was proposed to *lower* the wages to just *six* shillings per week, the men decided to make a stand. Led by George Loveless, a farm labourer who was also a local Methodist preacher, they formed a 'Friendly Society of Agricultural Labourers'.

Such an organisation was not against the law, but unfortunately in forming their society they held a ceremony in which they swore loyalty to each other. This was their undoing – for they were charged with 'administering unlawful oaths' – committing a breach of an obscure law which had been passed a few years earlier to deal with a naval mutiny.

In March 1834 all six men were charged, found guilty, and sentenced to seven years' transportation to the penal colony in New South Wales, Australia. Five of them went to Australia and George Loveless, their leader, was sent to Tasmania – Van Diemen's Land, as it was then called.

They may well have perished and become completely forgotten. However, the enormity of the injustice of their sentence was such that many people took up their cause, including the social reformers Robert Owen and Thomas Wakley. A groundswell of public opinion led to a gigantic public demonstration in London – the first of its kind – in which more than 30,000 people gathered in Copenhagen Fields, near where King's Cross station now stands. William Cobbett, Joseph Hume, Thomas Wakley and other MPs constantly raised the matter in parliament and a petition of over 800,000 signatures was presented. Eventually, in 1836, it was agreed that all the men should have a full and free pardon.

THE TOLPUDDLE MARTYRS

| JAMES BRINE | THOMAS STANFIELD | JOHN STANFIELD | GEORGE LOVELESS | JAMES LOVELES |
| AGED 25 | AGED 51 | AGED 25 | AGED 41 | AGED 29 |

The Tolpuddle Martyrs in an impression drawn on their return from Australia printed in Cleave's Penny Gazette of Variety, *1838. Unfortunately, James Hammett is not shown as he took longer to return home.*

Ironically, it was only by chance that George Loveless read of his pardon in a London newspaper that he happened to pick up as he was serving out his sentence in Tasmania. Even then, it still took some years before he and the others finally returned to England. James Hammett, slaving in Australia's outback, did not get back until 1839.

All except James Hammett migrated for a better life to Canada, near Ontario, where they prospered, and their descendants are still there today. Only James Hammett remained in England, to die in Dorchester's workhouse in 1891, aged seventy-nine. He is buried in Tolpuddle (see page 18).

THE REVEREND HENRY MOULE (1801–80) INVENTOR OF THE MECHANICAL EARTH-CLOSET

Dorchester County Museum is the proud possessor of an extraordinary gadget which would nowadays be called a portable loo. It was invented by the Revd Henry Moule, Vicar of Fordington from 1829 to 1880.

This was no ordinary loo, nor was Henry Moule an ordinary vicar. He wrote many books and pamphlets on religious and educational topics and also volumes of poetry. However, he claimed international fame for the invention of his mechanical earth-closet. He invented it, made it, marketed it, and made a small fortune selling it. The Indian Government bought them in large numbers for use in hospitals, lunatic asylums and gaols throughout Bengal, the Punjab and the North West Provinces. For these they paid Moule £500 – a considerable sum in those days.

In England his earth-closets were used in schools and the army camp at Wimbledon had fifty of them used daily by 200 men – 'without the slightest annoyance to sight or smell'.

His earth closet consisted of a commode with a bucket below the seat and a hopper behind it containing dry earth or ashes. A lever produced a measured amount of earth, and covered up the excrement and its smell. This was the time when Britain's growing population was producing an intolerable sanitary problem and cholera and other diseases were rife. Moule's loo was a brave attempt to ease the problem.

One of Henry Moule's sons, Horace, was a great personal friend of Thomas Hardy – living close by and just eight years younger.

SHE SELLS SEASHELLS

Even those who have never heard of Mary Anning have probably struggled in childhood to pronounce the tongue-twister: 'She sells seashells on the sea shore' – thus unwittingly quoting the jolly rhyme written in her memory. In fact, Mary Anning holds a uniquely important place in the gradual discovery in the early nineteenth century, of the Jurassic world of dinosaurs. Living in Lyme Regis, she made an immense contribution to palaeontology (see page 106).

The popular rhyme written by Terry Sullivan in 1908 was directly inspired by her life story. There is now a large and growing literature about her – especially now that dinosaurs have become a permanent craze among children and fans of *Jurassic Park*.

> She sells seashells on the seashore
> The shells she sells are seashells, I'm sure
> So if she sells seashells on the seashore
> Then I'm sure she sells seashore shells

(Original text, written in 1908 by Terry Sullivan, set to music by Harry Gifford.)

ALSO BORN IN DORSET

Anthony Ashley-Cooper (1621–83), born in Wimborne St Giles
Famous Royalist during the Civil War. Created Baron Ashley and then Earl of Shaftesbury. Helped to bring Charles II back to the throne.

Thomas Bell (1792–1880), born in Poole

Naturalist, dental surgeon, professor of Zoology at King's College and lecturer in anatomy at Guy's Hospital. Also president of the Linnean Society.

Anthony Blunt (1907–83), born in Bournemouth

Art historian and Soviet spy. Cambridge-educated friend of Guy Burgess, Kim Philby, and Donald Maclean. Stripped of his knighthood for treason in 1979. Blunt was born while his father was Vicar of Holy Trinity Church, Old Christchurch Road (now destroyed).

Verney Cameron (1844–94), born in Weymouth

Famous Victorian explorer. First European to cross Africa coast to coast. Surveyed Lake Tanganyika. Rescued the remains of David Livingstone.

John Le Carré (1931–), born in Poole.

Novelist. Formerly served in the British Foreign Service. Inventor of Smiley.

Christopher Chataway (1931–), born in Sherborne

Pace-maker for Roger Bannister when he ran the first sub-4-minute mile. Set world record for the 5,000 metres in 1954. Became the first BBC Sports Personality of the Year in 1954. Newscaster, politician. Knighted in 1995.

Ethelbald (*c.* 834–60), born in Sherborne

A King of Wessex and an elder brother of Alfred the Great. Ethelbald reigned for only two years, 858–60, and when died he was buried in Sherborne Abbey. He had shocked his contemporaries by marrying his father's fifteen-year-old widow, Judith.

Percy Gilchrist (1851–1935), born in Lyme Regis

Metallurgist, who successfully worked on new methods of steel production.

John Gould (1804–81), born in Lyme Regis

Ornithologist, artist and publisher, who wrote and illustrated eighteen books of bird illustrations, including those of Asia and

Australia. Aged just twenty-three, he became the first Curator of the Museum of the Zoological Society in London. The Gould League in Australia is named after him (see page 31).

Radclyffe Hall (1880–1943), born in Bournemouth
Poet and novelist, famous in the 1920s and '30s for her scandalous lesbian novel *The Well of Loneliness*, published in 1928 (see page 32).

Alexander Hood (1727–1814), born in Thorncombe
Naval commander.

Samuel Hood (1724–1816), born in Thorncombe
Naval commander. The two Hood brothers were famous and successful commanders during the many engagements with the French in the Napoleonic Wars. Both were made viscounts.

James Meade (1907–95), born in Swanage
Economist and Nobel Prize winner.

Hubert Parry (1848–1918), born in Bournemouth
Composer and professor at the Royal College of Music. His most famous composition, 'Jerusalem', a setting of William Blake's poem, is virtually England's alternative national anthem.

Thomas Love Peacock (1785–1866), born in Weymouth
Novelist and poet. Worked with the East India Company. His books include: *Headlong Hall* (1816), *Nightmare Abbey* (1818), and *Crotchet Castle* (1831). A shrewd observer of human silliness.

Matthew Prior (1664–1721), born in Wimborne
Son of a joiner, he rose to become an influential diplomat and writer of witty, light verse.

Alfred Stevens (1818–75), born in Blandford
Son of a house-painter and decorator. Stevens was a remarkable sculptor, whose early talent was first noted by the rector of Blandford St Mary, Samuel Best, who sent the boy to Italy to study art. Stevens' most notable work is the Wellington memorial in St Paul's Cathedral, London.

Thomas Sydenham (1624–89), born in Wynford Eagle
Much respected seventeenth-century physician – so much so
that he was called 'The English Hippocrates'. Studied many
diseases scientifically for the first time. The childhood complaint
Sydenham's chorea, also known as St Vitus' Dance, is named after
him.

William Talbot (1800–77), born in Melbury Abbas
Physicist and pioneer of photography, inventing several new
techniques. His *Pencil of Nature,* published in 1844, was one of
the very first books to be illustrated by photographs.

James Thornhill (1675–1734), born in The White Hart Inn in Melcombe Regis (Weymouth)
A foremost baroque painter, whose works include the interior
dome of St Paul's Cathedral, Blenheim Palace, the painted hall
at Greenwich Palace, and the ceiling of the Queen's Bedroom at
Hampton Court. Knighted in 1720.

Virginia Wade (1945–) born in Bournemouth
Tennis player, winning three Grand Slam singles titles and four
Grand Slam doubles. Winner of Wimbledon's Women's Singles
title in 1977. TV tennis commentator.

Poole has provided *two* winners of the Miss World Contest:
Ann Sidney won it in 1964.
Sarah-Jane Hutt won it in 1983.

PEOPLE WITH DORSET LINKS

Christian Bale (1974–). The film actor Christian Bale was a pupil
at Bournemouth Grammar School for Boys when he landed the
part of Jim Graham in Steven Spielberg's *Empire of the Sun.* He
had to be given special tuition during his weeks on location.

'Capability' Brown (1716–83) is believed to have been responsible
for designing and building the new 'model village' of Milton
Abbas. He received £105 for plans for the village and he made
many journeys to Milton between 1773 and 1776.

Thomas Burberry, the man who invented the Burberry coat – a weatherproof coat made of gabardine – lived in Radipole during the First World War.

Max Bygraves OBE (1922–) was a long-term Bournemouth resident from 1970 until he moved to Australia in the 1990s.

Sir Winston Churchill, as a teenager, was almost killed after falling from a bridge over Alum Chine in Bournemouth. He was playing with his cousins, and tried to leap from the bridge to a nearby tree. He missed, fell, and was unconscious for three days.

Eleanor Coade (1733–1821) is almost forgotten today – but her closely-guarded secret method of making 'Coade stone' made her famous and wealthy. Coade stone was an artificial stone with astonishing strength and durability. It could be moulded easily and was used on many public buildings for ornamentation.

Her factory was on the site of the present Royal Festival Hall until she retired to Lyme Regis. Her house there – Belmont House – carries examples of Coade stone decoration on its façade. Two other easily seen examples of Coade stone are the large lion on the south bank at the end of Westminster Bridge, formerly painted red and guarding the entrance to Waterloo station, and the strikingly painted statue of George III on the seafront in Weymouth.

Eleanor Coade was unique in her entrepreneurial skills – an astonishing feat for a young widow at the time when she lived.

John Constable (1776–1837) and his newly-wedded wife spent their six-week honeymoon at Osmington, where he painted several views of Weymouth Bay. The most famous of these was a view from Osmington looking across to Weymouth and Portland.

Thomas Coram (1668–1751) was born in Lyme Regis. He was a shipwright by trade; went to America in 1693; settled in Taunton, Massachusetts; returned to England in about 1720 and planned and founded London's famous Foundling Hospital (1741) of which William Hogarth was a patron.

John Endecott (*c.* 1588–1665) sailed from Weymouth in 1628 to found another new colony in North America. He became governor of the Massachusetts Bay Colony five times from 1629 to 1665. He may have been born in Dorchester, but this is disputed, and Chagford, Somerset, also claims to be his birthplace.

Tony Hancock (1924–68) was brought up in Bournemouth from the age of three. His parents kept the former Railway Hotel in Holdenhurst Road. After his father died, Hancock's mother and step-father moved to keep what is now the Quality Hotel.

Benny Hill (Anthony Hawthorne Hill) (1924–92) was a Southampton evacuee in the Second World War who spent part of his schooldays at Bournemouth Grammar School for Boys. He was reputed to have been a very naughty boy in class.

Sir Fred Hoyle (1915–2001), one of the most significant figures in British astronomy, who invented the term 'Big Bang', retired to Bournemouth, where he died in 2001, aged eighty-one. He was commemorated by a Blue Plaque in 2009, the Year of Astronomy.

Anna Pavlova (1881–1931), the famous Russian ballerina, went to Abbotsbury to make an intensive study of swans, preparing herself for her role in *The Dying Swan*.

Sir George Somers (1554–1610) was the English colonist who took possession of the Bermuda Islands – which were then for a while called the Somers Islands. He may have been born in Lyme Regis but certainly his pickled body was brought back to be buried in Whitchurch Canonicorum. He had died 'of a surfeit in eating of a pig.'

J.R.R. Tolkien (1892–1973), author of *Lord of the Rings*, was particularly fond of Bournemouth and he and his wife regularly spent weeks there at their favourite hotel, the Miramar, with its superb cliff-top view. He worked on *The Silmarillion* while staying there. He later retired to Bournemouth, but when his wife died he returned to Oxford, where he had been Professor of Anglo-Saxon. He died in Bournemouth, while visiting a friend.

Virginia Woolf (1881–1941). In 1910, Virginia Steven, as she then was, took part with her brother and a few friends in an extraordinary hoax, pretending to be Abyssinian princes. Fooling the Commander-in-chief of the Home Fleet, they boarded HMS

Dreadnought in Portland Harbour and inspected a Guard of Honour. Wearing a black moustache and a beard, Virginia passed herself off as 'Prince Sanganya' and convincingly spoke gibberish.

Sir Christopher Wren was MP for Weymouth in 1702. It suited him as he was constantly coming to oversee the work in the Portland quarries, for building St Paul's Cathedral.

PEOPLE REMEMBERED BY DORSET STATUES

Lord Baden-Powell can be seen sitting on Poole Quay, looking towards Brownsea Island, the site of the first Scout camp. It is a fascinating life-size statue showing the founder of the Scout Movement sitting as if by a camp fire, with a couple of tree-stumps each side of him. He is dressed in his familiar Scout uniform and hat. Passers-by can sit beside him and have their photos taken. The sculptor was David A. Annand. A plaque beside the statue reads:

> Robert Baden-Powell, O.M.
> 1st baron of Gilwell and Freeman of the Borough of Poole
> Founder of the Scout Movement
> Poole – where it all began

William Barnes (1801–86) stands on a plinth outside St Peter's church in Dorchester. It is a strikingly life-like statue, showing him dressed in his long coat just as he would have appeared walking around the town and going to the school he ran for local boys in South Street.

Christopher Crabbe Creeke (1820–86) is shown sitting on a loo outside the Bournemouth International Centre. Importantly, he was Bournemouth's first Inspector of Nuisances, and so worked on the town's sanitary arrangements – hence the loo. He is shown sitting in a pensive mood.

This statue, by Jonathan Sells of Corfe, is much used as a photographic background by students of Bournemouth University after they have received their degrees in the adjacent International Centre.

George Loveless (1797–1874), the leader of the six Tolpuddle Martyrs, is shown sitting on a bench at the entrance to the Memorial Cottages in Tolpuddle. It was commissioned in 2000 by the TUC and executed by Thompson Dagnall. Loveless is shown in despair at the time he was in Dorchester prison, held behind while his five fellow Martyrs had already been put on board the hulks. The sculpture, made from Portland stone, is designed for visitors to sit alongside him. At the back of the seat are six blocks of stone, one for each Martyr, on which are carved words from the trial – including Loveless's own famous phrase: 'We will, we will, we will be free.'

This sculpture of George Loveless by Thompson Dagnall is at the entrance to the Memorial Cottages in Tolpuddle. Loveless is shown sick and in despair, waiting to be transported to Australia.

George III (reigned 1760–1820) who brought fame and prosperity to Weymouth and who popularised the very notion of holidaying at seaside resorts, has the most colourful statue in Dorset – on the seafront at Weymouth. The statue was 'raised by the grateful inhabitants . . . on his entering the 50th year of his reign.' It is made of Coade stone, an artificial material which is astonishingly weather-resistant. Mrs Eleanor Coade, who developed the recipe for Coade stone, lived at Lyme Regis.

Captain Lewis Tregonwell (1758–1832) is remembered in the most unusual statue in Dorset – or arguably anywhere else for that matter. In fact it is a double statue, together with Christopher Crabbe Creeke, described on page 137. Tregonwell is generally considered to be the 'founder' of Bournemouth, having built the first private house there in 1810, and first occupied it in April 1812.

Whereas Christopher Crabbe Creeke is sitting on a toilet seat, Tregonwell is standing behind him, holding a bucket and spade in one hand, as symbols of Bournemouth's reputation for a premier seaside resort. In his other hand he holds a scroll on which are the names of three locally born holders of the Victoria Cross.

Thomas Hardy (1840–1928) has his famous bronze statue, sculpted by Eric Kennington, at the top of Dorchester's High Street. Hardy is seen looking away from the town, and gazing towards his beloved Wessex. Flowers appear at his feet on the anniversaries of his birthday (2 June) and the day of his death (11 January).

Dorset Martyrs' Memorial in Dorchester, is on the site of the old town gallows, and comprises a group of three bronze figures by Dame Elisabeth Frink. It commemorates all those local martyrs who died for their religious beliefs in the sixteenth and seventeenth centuries. It was placed here in 1986.

Two naked figures, slightly larger than life-size, stand facing a mysterious third figure, vaguely draped, who is clearly either an executioner or a personification of Death itself. They are all standing at ground level, and passers-by can walk around and between them, so that they appear real – not at all like statues perched high on pedestals apart from life.

The Bishop of Salisbury suggested the wording on a plaque set in the ground in the centre of the group. It was crafted by Michael Harvey of Bridport. The words are:

FOR CHRIST AND CONSCIENCE SAKE

Although these figures stand for all victims of hideous intolerance, they also refer more specifically to seven Catholics executed at the Dorchester gallows in 1594, gruesomely hanged, drawn and quartered.

11

SKIRMISHES & WAR

No major battle has taken place in Dorset, though the last battle to take place in England – Sedgemoor – was just over the border in Somerset. Nevertheless, there have been countless skirmishes and military events over the years. The Romans and the Vikings were the first disturbers of Dorset's peaceful existence.

Probably the earliest major skirmish to take place in Dorset was fought shortly after the Romans arrived in Britain in the first century AD – and it took place at Maiden Castle, just outside Dorchester, where archaeological finds suggest that this hill fort, defended by the Celts, lost out to the superior military might and expertise of the Roman army.

The Danes made frequent raids up the River Frome in the ninth century. The town walls at Wareham were built in AD 876, perhaps by King Alfred the Great himself, to defend the town against these Danish attacks. The Danish forces suffered a huge setback in 877, when a great fleet of their ships transporting soldiers sailed westwards from Poole. It is recorded that a severe storm struck the fleet off Swanage, resulting in the sinking of 120 ships. If you reckon that each Viking longship was carrying 30 men, this means that the Danish army lost about 3,600 fighting men. To King Alfred, this must have seemed like an act of providence.

In Swanage today there is a King Alfred Monument on the promenade next to the seashore. It is a tall stone pillar commemorating this event – seen as a victory for King Alfred. Somewhat anachronistically, the top of the column is surmounted by cannon-balls!

'RED BOTTOM'

Ethelred the Unready (reigned 978–1016) provoked the Danes by breaking a treaty with them in 1002 and massacring large numbers of Danish men, women and children. Understandably, the Danes were incensed, and in revenge they killed, raped and pillaged all along the south coast.

However, when the Danes attempted to invade Burton Bradstock, pushing into the inlet now called Burton Freshwater, the Burton folk were ready for them. The Danes were slaughtered to a man and the whole area ran red with their blood. The dip in the hill where the action took place is still known locally as 'Red Bottom'.

FIRE BEACONS TO WARN OF THE ARMADA

Melbury Hill, 800ft above sea level, is the site of one of the string of fire beacons lit across the country to warn of the Spanish Armada in 1588. Fire beacons were the perfect way of communicating the danger signal, and as the Armada sailed its way up the English Channel, these coastal fires were quickly followed by inland fires. Melbury Beacon swiftly summoned the Wiltshire Militia to march to Weymouth to be ready for possible action.

400 years later, on 19 July 1988, the beacon was lit again, to commemorate the anniversary of the arrival of the ill-fated Spanish Armada.

THE LOUDEST BANG EVER HEARD IN DORSET

No one could have counted the decibels – but surely the destruction of Corfe Castle by gunpowder in 1646 must have been heard for many miles around. An anonymous writer at that time, calling himself 'Mercurius Rusticus', wrote an account of the siege and the way the Parliamentarian forces used the village church at Corfe as their battery:

> The first time the rebels faced the castle they brought a body of between two and three hundred horse and foot, and two pieces of ordnance, and from the hills played on the castle, fired four houses in the town, and then summoned the castle; but receiving a denial for that time they left it . . . But on

three-and-twentieth of June . . . with a body of between five and six hundred, came and possessed themselves of the town . . . They brought with them to the siege a demi-canon, a culverin, and two sacres; with these and their small shot they played on the castle on all quarters of it with good observation of advantage, making their battery strongest where they thought the castle weakest. . . .

The most advantageous part of their batteries was the church, which they without fear of profanation used, not only as their rampart but their rendezvous; of the surplices they made two shirts for two soldiers; they broke down the organ and made the pipes serve for cases to hold their powder and shot; and not being furnished with musket-bullets, they cut off the lead of the church and rolled up and shot it without ever casting it in a mould.

Despite all their attempts, Corfe Castle continued to defy the besiegers, and the occupants, led by Lady Bankes, held the castle for many months. It was only as a result of treachery that Corfe Castle was finally captured. Lady Bankes and her family were allowed to leave, and then, because the castle was obviously so important and impregnable, the House of Commons voted to demolish it.

The Parliamentarians were determined to blow it up. They spent nine months digging tunnels under the walls and filled these with massive amounts of gunpowder. When, finally, they detonated the powder, huge parts of the castle simply sank into the excavations beneath, and other sections rolled down to the bottom of the hill. The explosions must have shattered the ears of all who witnessed this horrendous destruction.

During the siege of Corfe, the Parliamentarian forces stripped the roof of Lulworth Castle of its lead, to make extra musket balls.

LYME'S HEROIC DEFENCE OF 1644

During the Civil War the citizens of Lyme Regis were staunch Parliamentarians. From April to June 1644, they were heroic in defending themselves against a siege led by Prince Maurice, the nephew of King Charles I. The Royalist army stormed the town three times without success, losing 2,000 men in their attacks.

During the siege, the women of Lyme dressed themselves up in trousers, so as to make the Royalists think they were men. They stoutly helped to bring ammunition up to the front line of the defenders. Meanwhile, Parliamentarian ships helped them by bringing supplies, braving the Royalist bombardment of the harbour.

Their bravery paid off, and when Prince Maurice heard that a Parliamentarian army led by the Earl of Essex was on its way to relieve the siege, he recognised that he was beaten.

Early on the morning of 15 June, he withdrew his army towards Exeter 'with some loss of reputation for having lain so long with such a strength, before so vile and untenable a place, without reducing it.'

BULLET-HOLES IN A PULPIT

Abbotsbury was staunchly Royalist during the Civil War, so a party of Roundheads marched from Dorchester under their commander, Sir Anthony Ashley Cooper, to bring them to heel. Some of the Royalists, led by Colonel Strangways, tried to hold out in St Nicholas' church, but after a six-hour fight they had to surrender.

Two bullet-holes are still to be seen in the church's Jacobean pulpit as a reminder of this dramatic moment.

'CLUBMEN' SLITHER AWAY
ON THEIR BOTTOMS

Shaftesbury was the scene in the summer of 1645 of a somewhat shambolic battle between 'Clubmen' and Cromwell's forces. The Clubmen were mostly country yokels who were fed up with the disturbances of the Civil War, and determined in a rather haphazard way to do battle. They had no leader and no weapons, except pitchforks, clubs, and whatever farm tools they could find. After about 5,000 of them had been routed in Shaftesbury – slithering in panic down Gold Hill – they regrouped with about 2,000 men on Hambledon, one of the many hill forts constructed by the ancient Britons.

In its time Hambledon was probably defended against Romans, Saxons and Danes. However, this final encounter saw the end of the Clubmen, as again they slithered on their bottoms down the hilly slopes. Cromwell was contemptuous, recording that his army overcame them 'after a short dispute' in which his men 'killed not twelve of them, but cut very many.' Many Clubmen were taken prisoner, initially being held captive for the night in the church at Shroton. Among the captives were no fewer than four vicars and curates!

THE BLOODY ASSIZE

The terrible aftermath of the Battle of Sedgemoor, 1685, was the 'Bloody Assize' held in Dorchester, to put on trial all those who had taken part in the rebellion by the Duke of Monmouth to oust his uncle, James II. The judge was the notorious foul-mouthed sadist, George Jeffreys and it was the most savage assize in English history. A total of 312 prisoners were tried. The court was hung with scarlet 'to indicate a bloody purpose' and Judge Jeffreys made it plain from the outset that the only chance of obtaining pardon or respite was to plead guilty. Nevertheless, 292 received the sentence of death. In Dorset alone, the punishments were:

Executed	74
Transported	175
Fined or whipped	9
Discharged	54

In many cases, the only charge brought against these victims of the 'Bloody Assize' was that they had been 'absent from their habitations from and att the tyme of the Rebellion.'

PLANNING THE 'GLORIOUS REVOLUTION' IN DORSET

Charborough House, between Sturminster Marshall and Bere Regis, was the meeting-place in 1686 of a group of conspirators who were to change the course of English history. They were planning to overthrow 'the tyrant race of Stuarts' and their bold scheme was to oust James II from the throne and replace him with the Dutch Stadtholder, William of Orange.

The host on this occasion was Thomas Erle (1650(?)–1720), MP for Wareham and Deputy Lieutenant for Dorset. He led an incredibly active life, fighting in many battles, including the Battle of the Boyne in 1690.

The plans discussed at Charborough House led directly to the 'Glorious Revolution' of 1688 and the establishment of William III and Mary II as joint monarchs.

DORSET HELPS TO BEAT THE FRENCH AT QUEBEC

General Wolfe used the slopes of Hambledon Hill as a training ground for his men before embarking for Canada and storming the Heights of Quebec.

THE NAPOLEONIC WARS – DID 'BONEY' COME TO DORSET?

A fascinating Dorset tradition is that during the Napoleonic Wars no less an important trespasser landed on the coast near Lulworth than Napoleon Bonaparte himself.

Thomas Hardy, who loved to collect old legends and tales, wrote about this in his short story *A Tradition of Eighteen Hundred and Four,* in which 'old Solomon Selby' tells how, as a boy, he saw 'Bonaparty . . . the Corsican ogre' one night as he was helping to look after lambs on his father's Dorset farm.

Was it possible? Was it true?

A curious corroboration came from an unlikely source in the 1930s in a publication called *Dorset Up Along & Down Along* produced by the West Lulworth Women's Institute. In it, a member of the WI told how in her youth she had spoken to a French-speaking Dorset farmer's wife who claimed in her own youth to have seen Napoleon walk ashore near Lulworth. She was near enough to have seen him studying a map, which he then rolled up and muttered to his companion the word 'impossible'. The old woman who made this claim lived to be 104, so she would have been about twenty in 1804, when the incident is alleged to have happened.

DORSET AND THE SECOND WORLD WAR

The Lifetime War Sacrifice of Tyneham
One of the many sacrifices to help win the Second World War was made by all 250 inhabitants of Dorset's coastal village of Tyneham. In 1943, as the army was preparing for D-Day the following year, everyone in the village – men, women, and children – were given just three weeks to clear out of their homes, so that American tank crews could practise their manoeuvres among the houses and buildings there.

The day for their departure was fixed for six days before Christmas. Although they were told that sometime in the future they would return, in fact the village has been left abandoned for good ever since that time.

As they left, a Sunday School teacher, Helen Taylor, pinned a poignant little note on Tyneham's church door. It read:

> We have given up our homes where many of us lived
> for generations to help win the war to keep men free.
>
> We shall return one day and thank you for treating the
> village kindly.

On 25 January 2010, the last living inhabitant of Tyneham, Arthur Grant, aged eighty-seven, was buried in Tyneham churchyard – it was his dying wish to return to Tyneham, where he attended the village school and pumped the organ in St Mary's Church. His relatives found his coat-peg in the village school – still with his name against it.

The Dam-Busters. Barnes Wallis, the inventor of the bouncing bomb which breached the Möhne Dams in the Ruhr during the Second World War, used the inshore Chesil Beach Bombing Range to test its effectiveness.

More than 100 enemy aircraft were spotted off Portland on Thursday 15 August 1940. The ensuing air-fight resulted in many losses on both sides. Two New Zealand Spitfire pilots lost their lives: Terence Lovell-Gregg, with his plane on fire, managed to glide his Spitfire to Warmwell, but tragically crashed before he could make a landing. Pilot Cecil Hight fought in the skies over Bournemouth, but his when his plane was on fire he bailed out. Wounded, he failed to pull the ripcord of his parachute, and fell to his death in a private garden in Bournemouth's Leven Avenue. There is a 'Pilot Hight Road' in Bournemouth, named in his memory.

Portland Harbour was the principal setting-off point for the US 1st Infantry on D-Day. Tragically, these soldiers were bound for Omaha Beach, which saw the bloodiest fighting and the heaviest losses – 3,000 US troops killed on that first day of the invasion.

Studland Beach was used as an area for practising the D-Day invasion of Europe. Many of these rehearsals were deadly affairs using live ammunition – and pieces of ammunition are still being found there today.

Poole Harbour was the embarkation port for troops on D-Day in Operation Overlord. To mark this event, a 1.5-tonne terracotta plaque was created in 1994 by Poole Pottery to mark the fiftieth anniversary of the invasion of Normandy. During rebuilding work on the quay it was 'lost' for nine years, but was triumphantly returned to Dolphin Quays, restored, and re-dedicated on 11 November 2009.

Weymouth was targeted by German bombers because of the port activities and troop movements. There is a memorial in the town to record that between 6 June 1944 and 7 May 1945 no fewer than 517,816 British and American troops embarked from this port, together with 144,093 vehicles. Many hundreds of houses were destroyed or damaged by incendiary bombs, explosives and landmines. One 'oil-bomb' is recorded.

BRIDGING MOTHER SILLER'S CHANNEL AND MUCH MORE BESIDES

At the entrance to Christchurch harbour is a boggy area known as Stanpit Marsh, nowadays valued as a nature reserve, but in former times much frequented by smugglers. Anyone walking here will notice a small metal bridge crossing the inlet called 'Mother Siller's Channel'.

It's easy to take this construction for granted – but its historical importance in helping to win the Second World War is immense. The somewhat neglected-looking little bridge at Stanpit Marsh is the prototype of the original Bailey Bridge and it is the oldest of the very few remaining Second World War Bailey Bridges.

Donald Bailey, who invented this type of bridge, was a civil servant working at the Military Engineering Experimental Establishment (MEXE) at Christchurch. As a hobby he liked designing bridges, and this famous design – known universally as the Bailey Bridge was made up of pre-fabricated sections very much like large pieces of Meccano. The sections were simple, flexible in use, easy to transport and construct, and their value in making incredibly quick work of crossing rivers made them vitally important during the recapture of Europe after D-Day.

Writing after the war, Field Marshal Bernard Montgomery wrote:

> Bailey Bridging made an immense contribution to ending World War II. As far as my own operations were concerned, with the Eighth Army in Italy and with the 21 Army Group in North West Europe, I could never have maintained the speed and tempo of forward movement without large supplies of Bailey Bridging.

A section of the original Second World War Bailey Bridge prototype. It is one of a pair of sections across Mother Siller's Channel in Stanpit Marsh, Christchurch. It was designed and built locally in Christchurch.

A single section of a Bailey Bridge can easily be seen displayed beside a roundabout on the road between Bournemouth and Christchurch, preserved as a memorial to Donald Bailey. The roundabout itself is just across the road from what used to be the military establishment where Donald Bailey developed his ideas – but this area is now a small trading estate.

12

GHOSTS & OLD TALES

Strange, quaint and amusing, here are some of the Dorset tales which have been told down the centuries in many an ingle-nook and over many a pint of well-brewed ale. . .

Legend has it that it was St Augustine who founded the former abbey at Cerne – just below the hill where the Cerne Giant is waving his club and displaying his manhood. What the old monks must have thought of him is best left to the imagination.

Augustine's first attempts to convert the old inhabitants of Cerne were met with scorn and derision, and he and his missionaries had cows' tails pinned onto the backs of their habits. The saint got his own back, however, and to their embarrassment the villagers of Cerne grew tails themselves, and for a while all future generations at Cerne were also born with tails.

Another legend tells how St Augustine gave the village its well. He asked the locals whether they wanted beer or water – and when they tactfully opted for water he struck the ground and created a well for them. The abbey has long disappeared, but St Augustine's well still exists there.

The giant himself at Cerne Abbas also has his share of legends. It was believed by the locals that he was a real ogre who ravaged the land around Cerne, particularly annoying farmers by stealing their sheep. At last, helped by the fairies, the local inhabitants managed to capture him, flatten him out, and then permanently pin him down on a convenient hillside.

Yet another legend tells that there is a secret passage running between Cerne Abbey and Cat-and-Chapel Hill – the hill that goes to the village of Piddletrenthide. On this hill was a chapel dedicated to St Catherine, the patron saint of unmarried girls. Inevitably, a stream of young women would make their way to this chapel with a special prayer to the saint:

Sweet Catherine, send me a husband.
A good one, I pray:
But arn a one better than narn a one,
O, Saint Catherine, and
Lend me thine aid
And grant that I never may
Die an old maid

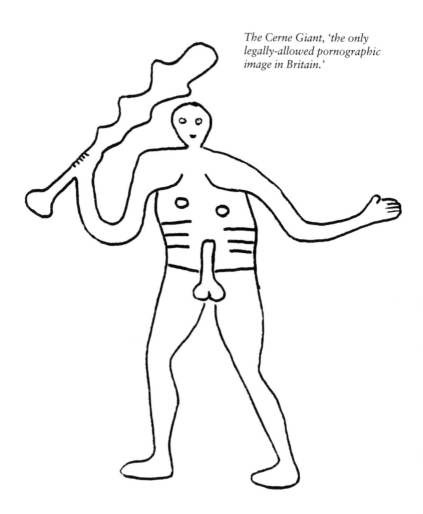

The Cerne Giant, 'the only legally-allowed pornographic image in Britain.'

(The odd name, 'Cat-and-Chapel' is almost certainly an abbreviation of 'Catherine').

Arguably, the Cerne Giant still possesses magical and powerful aphrodisiacal powers in the most important part of his anatomy. Lovers who linger on that spot are convinced that the giant's potency will enhance their own. Quite recently a well-known titled member of the aristocracy and his wife were so successful in their endeavours that they named their resulting daughter Cerne, in happy gratitude.

WITCHES

Well into the twentieth century witches were a constant dread among Dorset folk, who did their best to ward off the evil eye. Putting a dead cat or a pig's head stuffed with pins into the thatch or chimney of a cottage was thought to protect the occupants against the power of witches A mummified cat was found in the roof of a cottage at Marnhull, with a mummified mouse in its jaws. Meanwhile, a bullock's heart filled with nails, pins and thorns was found in a chimney near Bridport.

Horseshoes placed over doorways were widely believed to be effective in bringing good luck and fending off spirits. In Dorset, china dogs on the mantlepiece were also thought to be effective.

Within living memory at the beginning of the twenty-first century witches were thought to be able to 'overlook' their victims, who were then taken ill and rendered incapable. At Gillingham a man applied for Parish Relief, claiming that his sister-in-law had 'overlooked' him, and so he was unfit for work.

At Tarrant Rushton the villagers were afraid to walk past the house of a woman who they believed to be a witch. They would walk miles to avoid her. At Winterbourne Houghton all illnesses in the village were attributed to an old woman there who was obviously a witch – proved by the fact that she was the seventh child of a seventh child.

A common belief was that the best way to deal with a witch was to draw her blood. The folk at Houghton used to lay in wait for witches in the dark, and then leap out at them with knives to make them bleed. Hardy refers to this old belief in *The Return of the Native*, when Susan Nonsuch pricks Eustacia Vye with a needle to counteract the spell she was thought to have cast over Clym Yeobright.

Covens of witches used to meet near Cheselbourne. One of their meetings was disrupted by the local authorities, and in the affray which followed, a particularly powerful witch, Ann Riggs, was killed. She was buried outside the churchyard, but the villagers were somewhat guilt-ridden. They extended the walls of the churchyard to include her grave in the consecrated ground. Her gravestone can still be seen.

During her life, Ann Riggs was supposedly responsible for many Cheselbourne misfortunes – including the deaths of nine horses, which she had ridden to exhaustion on nine successive night rides.

THE 'SKIMMITY RIDE'

Readers of Hardy's *The Mayor of Casterbridge* will remember the scene when Lucetta suffers a fainting fit and later dies after seeing a crude stuffed effigy of herself on a donkey, paraded beneath her window, with the townsfolk jeering and cat-calling. The raucous affair was, of course, the 'skimmity-ride' which the *Oxford English Dictionary* defines as 'a ludicrous procession, formerly common in villages and country districts, usually intended to bring ridicule or odium upon a woman or her husband in cases where the one was unfaithful to, or ill-treated, the other.'

Old folk in Hardy's time could well remember this old custom, but it was quickly dying out by the time Hardy described it in his novel. The origin of 'skimmity' is that the woman in the procession used to be shown as beating her husband with a skimming ladle – just as present-day images of a bossy wife invariably show her to be wielding a rolling-pin.

THE DORSET OOSER

The hideous, frightening, pagan wooden mask known as the 'Dorset Ooser' was unfortunately lost at the end of the nineteenth century. Luckily, however, two photographs were taken of it, and a splendid modern replica can now be seen in the Dorchester County Museum. Before it was lost it belonged to a family at Holt Farm, Melbury Osmond, and was a feature in old village customs in that area.

The Dorset Ooser was a mask in the shape of a huge wooden face adorned with beard and shaggy hair, wild staring eyes, a row of fierce teeth, and with gigantic bull's horns projecting on each side. The mouth was hinged, so that the lower jaw could move and snap at onlookers much in the manner of old hobby-horses in medieval street processions.

Clearly, the Ooser was a final remnant of ancient pagan customs when men dressed themselves in animal skins and put on grotesque masks to be worn in traditional processions and dances. Nowadays, on May Day, the newly made replica is taken out of Dorchester Museum as a part of the procession of Morris dancers on top of the Giant's hill at Cerne Abbas – thus keeping alive something of the primitive practices that the Christian church tried so hard to suppress in earlier centuries.

The Dorset Ooser. Sadly the original has been lost but there is a modern version in the Dorset County Museum in Dorchester.

The original Ooser may well have represented the Devil, and it took part in the raucous happenings at 'Skimmity Rides' – fortunately preserved for memory by Thomas Hardy in *The Mayor of Casterbridge*.

A tale told in Melbury Osmond is that the Ooser was used to play practical jokes on children and even grown-ups, having chains attached and Lucifer matches pushed alight into the head. Once, when a young stable-lad was one of its victims the poor young man was so frightened that he jumped through a window and almost killed himself in his desperate panic to escape.

An old custom at Shillingstone was the 'Christmas Bull' – not unlike the Ooser. This was a man dressed up in a shaggy coat, with fearsome bull's head with glass eyes, and wearing large sharp horns. The bull and his keeper would make their appearance at any time in any house, wherever there were Christmas celebrations. They were allowed to go anywhere they wanted within that dwelling. Occupants of the houses would flee before him – especially as the bull and keeper became progressively well-oiled by ales or wines as the evening wore on. The custom lasted into the twentieth century.

THE GHOST OF A HEADLESS FEMALE SAINT

One of the weirdest stories about medieval saints concerns St Juthwara, otherwise known as St Judith. Legend has it that she lived in the Dorset village of Halstock in the seventh or eighth century – possibly a Celtic noblewoman.

The Oxford Book of Saints unkindly suggests that these legends are 'a farrago of impossibilities' – but who are we to judge? Apparently Juthwara suffered from chest pains, and went to her wicked stepmother to ask her advice. The stepmother helpfully recommended applying two fresh cheeses to her breasts, and then, wicked as ever, she then told her even wickeder son, Bana, that Juthwara was pregnant.

Bana immediately stripped off Juthwara's underclothes and found that her bra was wet – obviously a sign of something untoward . . . so naturally he swiped her head off with his sword. A spring of water miraculously appeared where the head fell. Calmly, Juthwara picked up her head, walked into Halstock church, and laid it on the altar.

Whoever Juthwara was, her relics were certainly taken to Sherborne Abbey during the time when Aelwold was bishop (1045–58) just before the Norman conquest, and she was greatly venerated there. Pilgrims used to come to her shrine until the Dissolution of the Monasteries under Henry VIII. Her feast day is 18 November, and her emblems are either a sword or a soft round cheese.

Juthwara's ghost has been seen on the hill where she is alleged to have been beheaded and in Halstock there is a field named after her. Until recently there was a pub named 'The Quiet Woman' with its sign showing a woman carrying her own head – but this pub has now become an excellent bed and breakfast guest house called Quiet Woman House.

OTHER GHOSTS AND POLTERGEISTS

In October 1969 a party of about a dozen boys were camping with two adults at Thorncombe Wood, close to Thomas Hardy's birthplace at Higher Bockhampton. One evening a terrified boy rushed to those in charge of the camp to say that he had just seen a ghost among the trees. He led a small and somewhat sceptical group to where he had seen the ghost, and all were amazed to see the figure of a Roman soldier, with shield, sword and helmet. The most astonishing thing about the apparition was that it was standing up in the air, about 2ft off the ground. One of the adults approached the ghost with a torch, but it simply melted away before their eyes. They realised later that it was standing on the site of the old Roman road from Dorchester to Badbury Rings – but on the level of the road as it was when the Romans built it, in the first century!

Day after day in August 1981, the *Bournemouth Evening Echo* was filled with alarming reports of the activities of a poltergeist which was making a great nuisance of itself in a house in Abbot Road in the Winton area of Bournemouth. Furniture flew through the air, ornaments were smashed, a biscuit barrel was hurled from one side of a room to another, cups and plates fell off the kitchen draining-board, the television lifted itself up and fell over, and the whole house was a wreck. All these events were witnessed by a police officer, who described how the temperature of the place dropped '10 to 15 degrees at least.' Attempts to exorcise the house failed miserably. The family fled, and the house was boarded up for months.

In the parish of Askerswell, near Bridport, in the late nineteenth century dozens of people went nightly to witness the regular supernatural happenings in a house there. The local rector, writing to *The Times*, described how huge pieces of rock were being thrown from one room to another – all apparently coming from the ceiling. The events ceased when a girl who lived there moved away to another house – which promptly burst into flames.

In August 1994, by the lodge gate between the main entrance to Kingston Lacy and Pamphill crossroads, Peter Giles, then a seventeen-year-old drummer, saw what he thought was a hitchhiker, but as he got closer he realised the figure was weirdly spectral. He described it as 'tall, wearing a white top hat and white gown down to his ankles and holding out a white stick like a blind person would. It was a really misty, transparent white but there was a solid edge to it.' His sister, Katrina, who was travelling with him, did not see it but felt a strong cold shiver at the time.

A former vicar, walking through Christchurch Priory, claimed to have seen a ghostly funeral procession of monks, taking a coffin from the priory to the graveyard outside. And the figure of a monk, thought to be John Draper, the last Prior of Christchurch, who died in 1552, has been seen several times at the entrance to the Draper Chapel. Other ghostly events in the priory include the smell of (non-existent) incense; and the sound of footsteps on a carpeted floor.

Christchurch has been hailed as a 'haunted hot spot' – with reports of ghosts being seen at Priory House, Ye Olde George Inn, the Regent Centre, the former Woolworths, the library, the Thomas Tripp pub, the Red House Museum, Soper's Lane, Christchurch Conservative Club, the Royalty Inn, the Bailey Bridge Hotel, the former Christchurch Barracks, Christchurch Hospital, the Salisbury Arms and Highcliffe Castle. And this is just a shortlist!

An unusual ghost which has reportedly been seen at Athelhampton House is that of a monkey. The story is that the unfortunate creature was accidentally shut up in a stairway by a girl who was about to commit suicide after being jilted by her lover. The ghostly monkey has not been seen recently, but other sightings of ghosts at Athelhampton include a lady in grey, two young men having a duel, a hooded monk and a cooper hammering away at phantom wine barrels.

The case of the Durweston poltergeist is a famous Dorset story – involving two young orphaned sisters who were taken from the local workhouse to live with a respectable woman, Mrs Best. Shortly after they arrived at Mrs Best's, strange scratchings and knockings began to be heard, and these noises became louder and louder until they were like hammer blows. Then stones and other objects began to lift themselves up and hurtle through the air. Many people came to witness the events, including a member of the Society for Psychical Research and it was clear that it was a classic case of poltergeist activity. The girls were moved to a home in Iwerne Minster, but the weird phenomena continued around them. The girls moved again, this time to London, but sadly one of them died shortly afterwards.

Durweston was also haunted by another ghost – the figure of a nurse – who used to walk in the garden of the present Rectory. The alarming legend about this spook was that if ever a child were to see it, then that child would die within a year. A bishop was asked to come and exorcise the spot, and after holy water had been sprinkled there, the nurse was never seen again. But did one of the girls at Mrs Best's catch sight of this nurse? That is something we shall never know. . . .

About five days before Christmas the 'White Donkey of Studland' makes its annual appearance. A white, spectral donkey has been seen wandering here by several people. It is believed to have belonged to an old smuggler carrying brandy, who was murdered by a naval deserter. The donkey fled, only to reappear in ghostly form.

The ghost of a headless woman has been seen many times over many years standing on the road leading to the main gateway of Corfe Castle. Who she is or was no one can tell. She simply stands, silently, by the broken stones.

The Duke of Monmouth haunts the road from Uplyme to Yawl. He rides a white horse, and appears about midnight, sometimes at the head of a group of his followers.

The ghost of Lawrence of Arabia, dressed in his Arab robes, has been seen by many visitors to his cottage at Cloud's Hill. He is seen quietly entering the cottage, and those who follow him are puzzled to find that the figure has completely disappeared.

The ghost of Sir Walter Raleigh, courtier, soldier, explorer and favourite of Elizabeth I, is said to return to 'Sir Walter Raleigh's seat' at the Old Castle at Sherborne at midnight on Michaelmas Eve. He walks among the trees before returning to his seat.

At Pimperne a ghostly severed hand appears. It's desperately trying to get reunited with the arm it belongs to – but sadly it won't find it, because the rest of the body is buried 90 miles away in London. It belonged to a poacher named Blandford, who was involved in a fight with game keepers in the late eighteenth century. In the fight, his hand was cut off. He was captured and sent to prison, later released, and went to live in London. His hand, however, was buried in Pimperne churchyard. Since then, it has reappeared at the site of the skirmish – aptly named Bloody Shard Gate, near Bloody Field.

In 1965 a lorry crashed into a Mini on Sturminster Newton bridge, killing the car's three occupants. Some time later, a young man was crossing the bridge on his motorbike when suddenly three figures stepped out in front of him. He could not brake, and to his amazement plunged straight through them. Looking back, he was unnerved to find that they had vanished.

During the desperate attempts to put out the fire which was raging at Lulworth Castle in 1929, one of the fire-fighters heard cries from the top of the castle and saw a lady evidently in distress in one of the tower windows. He quickly got help and ran up a ladder to rescue her – but when he got up to the window he found that the floor of the room had collapsed hours before. He realised that he had seen the 'Grey Lady', a ghost who had been haunting the castle for centuries.

THE TURBERVILLE GHOSTLY COACH
AND HORSES

On nights when there is a full moon, a spectral coach and horses leaves Woolbridge Manor to travel to the vanished Turberville mansion at Bere Regis. The chance of seeing it is strong if the full moon coincides with Hallowe'en. Hardy brings this old Turberville ghost-story into his novel, *Tess of the D'Urbervilles*.

Luckily (or perhaps unluckily) you can see this only if you have Turberville blood in your veins. In the 1960s a bus driver saw the phantom coach on the medieval bridge near the manor, and dutifully stopped his bus to let it go by. One wonders whether he was distantly related to the Turbervilles.

The manor house and bridge at Wool where the spectral coach and horses can be seen by those with Turberville blood in their veins.

13

THIS & THAT

Here is a selection of some Dorset-related oddments.

Rabbits must never be mentioned on the Isle of Portland. The islanders – especially the older inhabitants – regard them with such horror and misgiving that they refer to rabbits euphemistically as 'underground mutton' or 'long-eared furry things'. Portlanders associate rabbits with bad luck because apparently bunnies emerge from their burrows just before a rock fall. Quarrymen have been known to refuse to go to work once they see rabbits, believing that they cause landslides. The superstition came to light in 2005, when the Wallace and Gromit film *The Curse of the Were-Rabbit* was being shown. Special posters had to be made, omitting the word 'rabbit' and the film's title was changed to *Something Bunny is Going On.*

Portlanders are traditionally credited with being expert stone-throwers in defence of their 'island'. This led Thomas Hardy to invent the fictitious name for Portland – 'The Isle of Slingers'.

Onesiphorus Toop was the Rector of Bridport from 1682 to 1715. His strange name is taken from the second letter of Paul to Timothy, Chap. 1, v. 16–17 – 'The Lord give mercy unto the house of Onesiphorus; for he oft refreshed me. . . .'

Red squirrels are quite easy to find on Brownsea Island. Isolated, they live safely on the island, well away from the threat of grey squirrels.

A ducking-stool for naughty women is to be found in Christchurch, ready to plunge female culprits into the River Avon.

Billy Wilkins is one of the great trees of Dorset – a gnarled and knotty oak with a girth of 38ft – in Melbury Park estate, near Evershot. It is named after an estate manager of the early seventeenth century.

RAF pilots wiggle their wings when flying over lime trees in Parnham Park, near Beaminster. This is in memory of two airmen heroes, father and son, who are buried beneath them.

The spire of St Peter's church in the middle of Bournemouth is 202ft high, which is exactly half the height of the spire of Salisbury Cathedral.

Nudists can enjoy 800 metres of seashore along the coast at Studland, just west of Poole. It is considered to be one of the best nudist beaches in the country. They are warned, however, that there have been reports of 'unacceptable behaviour' among the sand dunes. Wardens keep a close watch on things.

The Blandford Fly is a small blackfly which can cause much havoc between April and June. After persistent efforts to control it, the Blandford Fly is less of a nuisance than it was in the 1980s. A report form is available for those who have been bitten.

Noddy's Toytown is said to have been inspired by the area round Studland. Enid Blyton lived nearby.

Little Willie is the name of the world's first tank – kept and displayed at Bovington Tank Museum. Little Willie was one of ten objects selected by the British Museum and the BBC from Dorset museums to tell the history of the world through 100 objects. The other nine objects were:

> Red Indian War Bonnet, (i.e. feathered head-dress) at the Russell-Cotes Art Gallery and Museum, Bournemouth
> Fossil extraction tool used by Mary Anning on the Jurassic Coast, at the Philpot Museum, Lyme Regis
> Poole Logboat, which dates to 295 BC, at Poole Museum
> The Swash Channel Wreck, a seventeenth-century merchant ship wrecked off Poole Harbour, whose remnants are in Poole Museum
> Valentine Cards – a collection of 400 cards from the Priest's House Museum, Wimborne
> Model Brewery, at the Dorset History Centre, Dorchester
> Ptarmigan Radio, the army's forerunner to the mobile phone, at the Royal Signals Museum, Blandford Camp

Roman ballista bolt, found embedded in a dead Briton
at Maiden Castle, at the Dorset County Museum,
Dorchester

Dry-earth loo. A mechanical dry-earth closet, patented in
1873 by the Revd Henry Moule of Fordington, at the
Dorset County Museum Dorchester (see page 130).

Naked rambler Stephen Gough from Bournemouth, was arrested
fifteen times during a ramble from Land's End to John O'Groats in
2003, wearing nothing but boots, socks, a rucksack and sometimes
a hat. In 2007, twenty naturist walkers were chaperoned in shifts
for 20 miles along the Jurassic Coast to Lulworth Cove.

Baptisms were sometimes oddly performed in rural Dorset. When
Henry Moule, inventor of the mechanical earth-closet, arrived at
Fordington, Dorchester, in 1829 as a young vicar, he was surprised
at his first baptism to find that there was no water in the font. His
Parish Clerk explained that the previous parson 'never used no
water; he did spit in his hand.'

Polystyrene ospreys have been placed in man-made nests in a
nature reserve in the wildest part of Poole harbour. These artificial
eyries are complete with white paint droppings. It's hoped to
attract real ospreys and entice them to nest in this area.

Sea water was considered to have very special healthful
properties, especially at the time when George III was holidaying
in Weymouth. A speculator built a splendiferous shore bath there,
costing him £500, hoping to attract the king's attention. George
used it once, gave the builder five guineas, and never came back.

Special baths were developed in the nineteenth century supposedly
to cure a vast number of ailments, real or imaginary. The Mont Dore
Hotel in Bournemouth (now the Town Hall) offered many: electric
baths, gas baths, agitation baths, oxygen baths and others such
as ozone, pine needle, borax, hyssop, creosote, carbolic, lavender,
iodine, mercurial, and sulphur. The Mont Dore Hydro also offered
an expensive Sultan's Bath for the huge sum of five shillings.

Lightning struck an elm tree in Lyme Regis in August 1800, killing
three women who were sheltering beneath it. In the arms of one of
the women was a baby – Mary Anning, aged fifteen months who

survived to become the famous fossil collector (see page 106). Her survival was considered to be a miracle, and her lively intelligence was locally attributed to the force of the lightning.

Cabbages were introduced into England by Anthony Ashley, Earl of Shaftesbury, in 1539. He imported this important vegetable from Holland to grow on his estate at Wimborne St Giles. He and his wife are buried in the village church there, with splendid effigies on their tomb. To salute his culinary innovation, a cabbage lies at his feet.

Victorian post boxes with vertical slots are to be found at Holwell, Mudeford, and Milford on Sea.

An Edward VIII post box – a very rare item, as Edward VIII (later to become the Duke of Windsor) reigned for less than a year – is to be found at Canford Cliffs in Poole.

Hitler's desk is to be seen in the Dorset Regiment Museum in Dorchester.

Beech trees forming the long avenue in the road from Wimborne to Blandford, alongside the Iron Age hill fort of Badbury Rings were planted in 1835 by William John Bankes of Kingston Lacy as an anniversary gift to his mother. Sadly, these trees are now having to be lopped, cut down, and replaced for future generations to enjoy. Originally, 731 beeches were planted – 365/6 on each side of the road.

Millions of snowdrops make a superb sight in early spring in the grounds of Kingston Lacy. The National Trust opens the gardens and grounds on those special weekends when the snowdrops are at their best.

'Push-wainling' was the odd word coined by William Barnes for a kids' push-chair – nowadays usually called a buggy. Barnes hated new words based on foreign languages, and much preferred Anglo-Saxon to Latin or Greek. Whereas 'pram' or 'perambulator' was a Latin-based word, his own 'push-wainling' was an attempt to invent a Saxon equivalent. A 'wainling' presumably means a little baby who has been weaned, but the word doesn't appear in any dictionary.

The Lulworth Skipper is not, as one might suppose, a master mariner based near the famous Lulworth Cove, but an increasingly rare small brown-and-orange species of butterfly that is found in south Dorset. Wet summers have resulted in a disastrous fall in skipper numbers – a loss of 70 per cent from 1992 to 2010.

The Melbury Fire Beacon, lit to warn of the Spanish Armada, was also lit to celebrate the Silver Jubilee of George V in 1935 and of Elizabeth II in 1977. It was also lit to celebrate the marriage of Prince Charles to Lady Diana Spencer in 1981.

Olympic Gold Medallist Victoria Pendleton, who won her gold medal in the Beijing Olympics for cycling, is giving a new take on the Hovis 'boy-on-a-bike' advert on Gold Hill. She is to revive the iconic scene in which Shaftesbury's Gold Hill became irrevocably linked with the famous brand of brown bread.

Gold Hill's ancient wall is a Grade I listed ancient monument. Recently, clearing it of weeds growing in the stonework was such a crucially important task that it required a special study by English Heritage before it could be untaken.

Teflon tapes are used to strap geo-location devices to the backs of nightjars in Wareham Forest. The birds migrate 10,000 miles away to unknown locations in Africa. The trackers' microchips, developed by Biotrak Ltd in Wareham, can store 100 days of data, which are downloaded when the nightjars return, hopefully giving clues about where they have been. The Teflon tapes are so smooth that they do not cause rubbing on wing-joints or plumage.

'Kimberlins' is the name given by Portlanders to those who are not natives to the Isle of Portland.

'Grockles' is the name given by natives of Bournemouth to the many tourists and day-trippers who come to visit the town.

Camel-racing is a popular sport at Badbury Rings. Masters of Foxhounds from all over Dorset compete for a Golden Fez, which is presented to the winner on a red velvet cushion.

The Arab head dress, robe and silk undershirt worn by Lawrence of Arabia are now on display in the refurbished Ashmolean Museum in Oxford. Large wooden doors, which Lawrence brought back from Saudi Arabia to be installed next to his swimming pool at his Dorset home, are also now on display there.

A **'Martello Tower'** was built on St Catherine's Point at Canford Cliffs. However, this was never a 'true' Martello Tower built for serious military defence – it was built in about 1857 as a folly for the Branksome Park Estate. It has long disappeared, but its name is perpetuated in Martello Road and Martello Park in Poole, suggesting to visitors that a genuine Martello fort was built hereabouts.

Guides who show tourists round Dorchester's former crown court building and cells in Dorchester where the Tolpuddle Martyrs were tried and sentenced to transportation, went on strike themselves in April 2010, demanding a rise from £26 for an afternoon's work to £50. The West Dorchester Council offered £30, but said it could afford no more. Result: the nine guides went on strike. Nothing changes! But at least they were not transported.

An Abbotsbury swan was used by Jacob Epstein as a model for St Michael's wing on his statue on Coventry Cathedral.

Golden Cap is the name of the highest point of the cliffs above Lyme Bay. At 627ft above sea level, it is the highest point on the south coast of England.

Moss-gathering was once a major and thriving industry in the village of Okeford Fitzpaine. The villagers there – even the children helping – would send bundles of moss to the traders of Covent Garden. The 'mossers' would use special rakes, and the moss would be tied into bundles ready to be taken by train from Shillingstone railway station.

A raw calf's head was one of a number of weirdly-assorted items formerly paid to the Lord of the Manor of Gillingham by the townsfolk of Shaftesbury for the privilege of drawing water from the wells in Enmore Green at Motcombe. Other items included a penny loaf, a gallon of ale, a pair of laced gloves, and the astonishing creation known as the 'Byzant' (see next page).

NOTICE
DORSET
ANY PERSON WILFULLY INJURING
ANY PART OF THIS COUNTY BRIDGE
WILL BE GUILTY OF FELONY AND
UPON CONVICTION LIABLE TO BE
TRANSPORTED FOR LIFE
7 88 GEO 4 G 30 S 13   BY THE COURT
T FOOKS

This notice in cast iron is fixed to many Dorset bridges. It dates from the reign of George IV (1820–30). Transportation to Australia ceased in 1867.

THE BYZANT

Townsfolk of Shaftesbury paid for the water they took from the wells of Motcombe at an age-old annual ceremony held in May, usually on the Monday before Ascension Day. A procession left Shaftesbury for Motcombe, led by an official carrying a decorated calf's head with a purse of money in its mouth. He was followed by a man carrying the Byzant – a highly ornate bulbous-headed mace decorated with gold, jewels and peacocks' feathers. Then followed the mayor and town officials and finally the townsfolk singing and dancing along the way. Down in Motcombe, the gifts of money, beer, bread, gloves and calf's head were handed over in a symbolic ceremony. The Byzant was then handed back, and the people of Shaftesbury wended their way back home up Gold Hill. The Byzant can still be seen in Shaftesbury's Local History Museum.

Poachers used to hide deer carcases in an empty tomb in the churchyard of Sixpenny Handley. Isaac Gulliver is also known to have hidden his smuggled goods in this churchyard.

The tenor bell hanging in the church of All Saints at Wyke Regis weighs three quarters of a ton, and bears the inscription:

> Lord may this bell forever be
> A tuneful voice o'er land and sea,
> To call thy people unto thee

Little Green Men are to be found in many churches in Dorset: Child Okeford, Cattistock, Iwerne Minster, Bere Regis, Mappowder, Shipton Gorge, Winterborne Whitchurch and Sherborne Abbey. These are not of the alien spacecraft variety, but are leafy faces carved in odd nooks and corners – relics of old pagan tree-worship.

One of Dorset's Green Men, a twenty-first century version from the Jubilee Physick Garden, Wimborne.

Two gay male swans – both hatched in 2002 – have nested together for several years. They regularly form a nest together and sit on it, obviously expecting to lay eggs. They have no interest in female swans, and are long-term partners. They are the only gay swans among the 1,000 other heterosexual swans at Abbotsbury.

Pregnant seahorses seen in the sea at Studland indicate that there was a seahorse baby boom in 2008. Conservationists are worried that too much boating activity might destroy them, and ask boat owners to avoid areas where eelgrass grows – the seahorses' favourite habitat.

The African Queen – the famous film starring Humphrey Bogart and Katherine Hepburn – was partly filmed in Dorset. In some scenes, the river used is not the 2,920-mile River Congo, but Dorset's considerably shorter River Piddle.

14

ON THIS DAY

1 January 1915

During the Second World War, HMS *Formidable* was sunk in the bay near Seatown. The bodies of many British sailors were washed ashore.

8 January 1857

William Barnes gave 'A Lecture on the Atmosphere' to the Corfe Castle Mutual Improvement Society.

11 January 1906

The main lighthouse on Portland Bill shone out for the first time.

11 January 1928

Thomas Hardy died in the house he had designed for himself, Max Gate, just outside Dorchester.

16 January 1928

Simultaneous funeral services of Thomas Hardy: his heart at Stinsford, and his ashes in Westminster Abbey.

18 January 1832

Death of Captain Lewis Tregonwell, the 'founder of Bournemouth'. He is buried in St Peter's churchyard in the town.

20 January 1857

The Wilts, Somerset & Weymouth Railway extended to Weymouth from Thingley Junction and Westbury.

22 January 1931

The lead casket containing the bones of Edward, Saint and Martyr, was discovered in the ruins of Shaftesbury Abbey.

29 January 2010

Funeral of Arthur Grant, aged eighty-seven, in Tyneham churchyard. He was the last living inhabitant of this village, forced to abandon their homes in 1943.

2 February annually

Date of the former hugely popular Candlemas Fair in Dorchester.

5 February 1993

The massive chimneys of Poole power station were demolished.

10 February 1914

Thomas Hardy married his second wife, Florence Emily Dugdale, who had been his secretary for several years.

16 February 1892

Death of James Hammett in Tolpuddle, aged seventy-six, the only one of the six Martyrs to die and be buried in England.

16 February 1943

A German Dornier bomber was shot down over South Buckham Farm, near Beaminster, killing all of its four crew.

22 February 1801

William Barnes, Dorset poet, was born at Bagber, near Sturminster Newton, the son of a farmer.

24 February 1834

George Loveless was arrested at dawn, the first of the Tolpuddle Martyrs to be seized.

25 February 2008

Topping-out ceremony on the newly erected Clavell Tower, having been moved 82ft further inland.

27 February 1646

The Royalist-held Corfe Castle finally surrendered to the Parliamentary forces after a three-year-long siege.

27 February 1848
Sir Hubert Parry was born in Bournemouth, then little more than a small collection of houses in undeveloped heathland.

2 March 1893
From this date until 21 June there was barely an inch of rain at Corfe Castle. Christchurch suffered a drought for 42 days.

4 March 981
King Edward the Martyr was buried in Shaftesbury Abbey.

5 March 1646
A vote was passed in the House of Commons (dominated by Cromwell) to demolish Corfe Castle.

7 March 1870
The date on the perpetual calendar Thomas Hardy kept on his desk, permanently set at this date – the day in 1870 he met Emma Gifford for the first time. It is now in Dorchester Museum.

9 March 1847
Death of Mary Anning, of breast cancer, in Lyme Regis.

14 March 1836
Free pardon granted to the Tolpuddle Martyrs by the king.

14 March 1915
Corporal Cecil Reginald Noble of Bournemouth gained the VC at Neuve Chapelle. Sadly, it was awarded posthumously.

17 March 1834
Trial of the six 'Tolpuddle Martyrs' began in the Crown Court of the Shire Hall in Dorchester.

18 March 978
The Saxon King Edward the Martyr was murdered at Corfe Castle.

18 March 1539
The abbot and the last sixteen monks of Sherborne Abbey were expelled, following the Dissolution of the Monasteries. The Parish Register records: *Expulsio Monarchorum de Shurborne.* Thus ended centuries of Benedictine rule.

19 March 1834

The 'Tolpuddle Martyrs' were sentenced to seven years' transportation to Australia.

24 March 2003

The Earl and Countess of Wessex opened the Wimborne Jubilee Physick Garden.

29 March 1866

John Keble, religious writer and poet, died in Bournemouth.

31 March 1998

Lulworth Castle was formally reopened by Pam Alexander, the Chief Executive of English Heritage, which had carried out its remarkable restoration.

1 April 1974

Bournemouth and Christchurch and some adjoining villages were incorporated into Dorset, following the Local Government Act 1972. They were formerly in Hampshire.

2 April 1942

Weymouth suffered its worst air-raid. Twenty people killed.

5 April 1769

Birth of Vice Admiral Sir Thomas Masterman Hardy, whose monument is high on a hill near his home, where he died, at Portisham House in Dorset. He was implored by the dying Lord Nelson in the memorable words, 'Kiss me, Hardy.'

6 April 1943

Death of Bournemouth-born Lt. Col Derek Anthony Seagrim in Tunisia, having been wounded in battle late in the previous month. He had been awarded the VC for his bravery in action.

10 April 1941

A German bomber flew over Bournemouth and dropped the bomb which killed the poet Cumberland Clark.

14 April 1471
> Queen Margaret of Anjou, wife of Henry VI, landed at Weymouth with her son Edward, Prince of Wales, to help in the Wars of the Roses. Within weeks, the young Prince of Wales was to be killed at the Battle of Tewkesbury.

21 April 1822
> A smuggler from Wyke Regis, William Lewis, was 'killed by gunshot wound'.

23 April 1975
> The Jane Austen Garden at Lyme Regis was opened by Sir Hugh Smiley, Chairman of the Jane Austen Society.

1 May annually
> May Day dancing round maypoles takes place in Dorset: traditionally next to the Cerne Abbas giant, and also at Abbotsbury, Buckhorn Weston and Sturminster Marshall.

3 May 1782
> George III declared a free pardon to all seamen 'Be they smugglers or outlaws in jail or overseas' on condition that they joined the Navy. This must have been a joke among Dorset smugglers!

6 May 2008
> A 1,312ft section of the Jurassic Coast was destroyed after a landslip, which was the worst in 100 years.

13 May 1935
> Lawrence of Arabia was fatally injured in a motorbike accident near his home at Cloud's Hill.

13 May annually
> 'Garland Day' at Abbotsbury – an old custom of parading two garlands of wild and garden flowers through the village.

19 May 1935
> Death of Lawrence of Arabia, after his accident on 13 May.

20 May 1892

A great fire destroyed much of the village of Sixpenny Handley. In five hours about a third of the dwellings were gone.

21 May 1799

Birth of Mary Anning, fossil-finder, in Lyme Regis.

22 May 1893

Dan Godfrey's band played its first concert at Bournemouth's Winter Gardens – Britain's first municipal orchestra and the beginnings of the Bournemouth Symphony Orchestra.

25 May annually

Feast day of St Aldhelm, first Bishop of Sherborne.

27 May 1541

Execution of Margaret, Countess of Salisbury, at the Tower of London. Her beautiful chantry is in Christchurch Priory.

29 May annually

Oak Apple Day. The bell-ringers of Nether Compton ring the bells in Trent to commemorate the Restoration of the Monarchy in 1660. King Charles hid in Trent Manor, fleeing to France after the Battle of Worcester.

1 June 1847

The London & South Western Railway opened between Southampton and Dorchester.

1 June annually

Feast day of St Wite, sometimes called St Candida, who is buried in her own church at Whitchurch Canonicorum.

2 June 1840

Thomas Hardy was born in the Hardy family cottage at Higher Bockhampton, near Dorchester.

3 June 1898

Lord Kelvin and Lord Tennyson visited Marconi at Alum Bay on the Isle of Wight. They sent the first commercial radio message from there to Bournemouth.

4 June 1731

Most buildings in Blandford Forum were destroyed by fire, necessitating the rebuilding of virtually the entire town.

11 June 1685

James Scott, 1st Duke of Monmouth, landed at Lyme Regis to raise a rebel army against his uncle, King James II.

13 June 1837

George Loveless was the first of the Tolpuddle Martyrs to return home.

14 June 1685

Monmouth's rebel army was met at Bridport by the Dorset militia. After a short battle, the rebels retreated.

15 June 1644

The Royalist army besieging Lyme Regis fled ignominiously.

29 June 1885

Thomas Hardy and his wife Emma slept in their new home, Max Gate, for the first time. Hardy himself had designed it.

1 July 1978

The church clock at Stourton Caundle was finally completed with the addition of the large and small hands. It was the first time the clock had been complete in all its 250 years.

3 July 1940

The first German bomb to be dropped on Bournemouth in the Second World War landed in Cellar's Farm Road, Southbourne, damaging nineteen houses.

4 July 1594

Four Catholics were hanged, drawn and quartered at the Dorchester gallows, on the spot where the Dorset Martyrs' Memorial now stands.

4 July 1930

Opening of the new Town Bridge across the harbour at Weymouth.

7 July 1789
King George III took a dip in the sea at Weymouth. Fanny Burney recorded the event.

8 July 1685
The Duke of Monmouth, fleeing from the Battle of Sedgemoor, was found hiding in a ditch on Horton Heath.

10 July 1967
Electric through trains began between Waterloo, Southampton and Bournemouth.

12 July 1910
Charles Stewart Rolls, co-founder of the firm of Rolls-Royce, was killed in an air crash at Hengistbury Airfield, Bournemouth – the first Briton to be killed in a flying accident.

14 July 1789
King George III was enjoying a boat trip off Portland Bill just at the same time as the fall of the Bastille in Paris.

17 July 1956
The Old Crown Court in Dorchester's High Street, where the Tolpuddle Martyrs were tried and sentenced, was opened to the public, preserved exactly as it was at the time of the trial.

19 July 1988
Melbury Beacon was lit to commemorate the 400th anniversary of the coming of the Spanish Armada.

20 July 1923
The Prince of Wales (later Edward VIII) visited Hardy at Max Gate. Hardy's dog Wessex had to be locked up for the occasion.

20 July 1939
Death of Sir Dan Godfrey, founder of the Bournemouth Municipal Orchestra, aged seventy-one, buried in St Peter's churchyard, Bournemouth.

25 July 1762

The Great Fire of Wareham swept through the town. Over 130 houses and buildings were destroyed.

28 July 1685

Dame Alice Lisle gave shelter to two fugitives from the Battle of Sedgemoor, leading to her execution by order of Judge Jeffreys.

31 July 1833

Princess (later Queen) Victoria, aged fourteen, arrived at Weymouth with her mother and governess to begin a holiday tour of Dorset.

1–8 August 1907

The first Scout camp was held on Brownsea Island, for 21 boys of different social backgrounds. It was led by the then Lieutenant-General Baden-Powell. This began the Scout Movement.

9 August 1856

Martha Browne was hanged in Dorchester, the last woman to be publicly hanged in Dorset. Thomas Hardy, aged sixteen, witnessed the event.

13 August 2008

Statue of Lord Baden-Powell was unveiled on Poole Quay by James Fleming, vice Lord Lieutenant of Dorset.

15 August 1645

Sherborne surrendered to the Parliamentarian army.

15 August 1832

Charles Dale discovered the first specimen of the butterfly he would name the 'Lulworth Skipper', at Durdle Door.

15 August 1940

New Zealand Spitfire Pilot Cecil Hight was shot down over Bournemouth. His name is remembered in Pilot Hight Road.

25 August 1855

The last horse-drawn coach came through Cerne on its regular route between Bristol and Weymouth. The coming of the railway had made it redundant.

29–31 August 1929

A disastrous fire swept through Lulworth Castle, gutting the interior and leaving the building a roofless ruin.

31 August 1934

Six cottages and a museum were dedicated in Tolpuddle in memory of the six Tolpuddle Martyrs, marking the centenary of their transportation to Australia.

2 September 1939

Benny Hill, aged fifteen, was evacuated from Southampton to Bournemouth, where he was educated at the boys' grammar school. Reputedly, he was a very naughty boy there.

4 September 1966

The last weekend of timetabled steam trains took place between Wareham, Corfe Castle and Swanage (but see 28 November 2009).

5 September 1685

Judge Jeffreys began his 'bloody assize' in Dorchester, traditionally believed to have been held in the Oak Room of the former Antelope Hotel.

5 September 1745

Birth of Isaac Gulliver, Dorset's most famous smuggler.

7 September 1642

The Battle of Babylon Hill was fought between the Royalists of Sherborne and the Parliamentarians from Yeovil. The battlefield is near Bradford Abbas. Neither side won.

13 September 1822

Death of the smuggler Isaac Gulliver, aged seventy-seven.

14 September 1804

Jane Austen, on holiday, bathed in the sea at Lyme Regis.

17 September 2008

The Duke of Gloucester visited Highcliffe Castle to see the progress made in its restoration. It was his fourth visit since 2001.

20 September 1930

The grain ship *Madeleine Tristan* was driven ashore in Chesil Cove – one of more than 400 shipwrecks recorded in Portland waters since the seventeenth century.

22 September 1651

Fleeing from the Battle of Worcester, Charles II reached Charmouth and spent the night at the Queen's Armes Inn.

23 September 1651

Still on the run after his defeat at Worcester, Charles II reached the George Inn at Bridport. Being recognised, he travelled north and spent the night at a house at Boadwindsor.

25 September 1810

Bournemouth was 'born'. Louis Tregonwell's purchase of land there was completed on this date, and this is the official date celebrating Bournemouth's bicentenary in 2010.

29 September 1716

The first coal-fired lamp shone out to sea where Portland upper lighthouse now stands.

30 September 1820

John Keats wrote his sonnet *Bright Star* at Lulworth Cove.

30 September 1940

German bombing raid on Sherborne. Fortunately, the abbey was not damaged.

2 October 1958

Death of Marie Stopes, famous advocate of birth control. Her ashes were scattered off Portland Bill, near where she lived.

7 October 1886

William Barnes died at Winterbourne Came, where he had been the parish priest for the last twenty-five years of his life.

8 October 1940

A German bomb fell next to St Nicholas's church, Moreton, destroying the north wall and shattering all the glass.

10 October 1867

The last convict ship, the *Hougoumont,* sailed from Portland, transporting 62 Fenian prisoners to Australia.

26 October 899

Death of King Alfred, King of Wessex.

28 October 1824

Death of the Christchurch smuggler John Streeter.

29 October 1618

Sir Walter Raleigh, the owner of Sherborne Castle, was beheaded.

30 October 1912

Very private wedding of Lt-General Baden-Powell to Olave St Clair Soames, in St Peter's church, Parkstone, Poole. He was fifty-five and she was twenty-three.

2 November 2009

The artificial reef at Boscombe was officially opened. It is the only reef of its kind for surfers in Europe.

6 November 1935

The foundation stone of the old Pier Approach Baths on Bournemouth seafront was laid. The baths, opened in 1937, were replaced by the controversial Imax building in 1992 (two years and eight months late).

12 November 1035

King Canute (Cnut) died at Shaftesbury Abbey. He was buried in the old Saxon Cathedral in Winchester.

18 Nov–9 Dec 1907
The Kaiser, grandson of Queen Victoria, stayed as a visitor at Highcliffe Castle, recuperating from a period of nervous strain.

22 November 1857
Birth of Baden-Powell, founder of the Scout Movement.

23 November 1824
A huge sea-wave swept inland to engulf and entirely destroy the village of East Fleet, a former haunt of smugglers. It was the only village in the county to be destroyed by the sea.

27 November 1912
Sudden and unexpected death of Emma, first wife of Thomas Hardy. Her death led to some of Hardy's finest poetry.

27 November 1953
Death of T.F. Powys, author of *Mr Weston's Good Wine*.

28 November 2009
After forty-three years, a steam locomotive ran direct from Swanage to London, thanks to a huge effort by the Swanage Railway Trust.

29 November 1940
A Spitfire, taking off from Warmwell, crashed in Durweston Forest near Winterbourne Stickland. A memorial to the airman can be found there.

9 December 1833
The oath was taken by the Tolpuddle Martyrs – the act which led to their arrest and transportation.

15 December 1785
'Prinny' – the Prince of Wales who later became George IV – secretly married his mistress, Mrs Maria Fitzherbert. She had formerly been the wife of Edward Weld, of Lulworth Castle.

19 December 1943

The inhabitants of Tyneham were forced to leave their village forever, handing the village over to the military, for practising manoeuvres in readiness for D-Day in 1944.

21 December 1993

A UFO allegedly flew over Gould's Hill at 11.00 a.m.

27 December 1926

Death of Wessex, Thomas Hardy's much-pampered and ferocious dog. Its gravestone is to be seen at Max Gate.

29 December 1886

Margaret, Countess of Salisbury, whose chantry is in Christchurch Priory, was beatified by Pope Leo XIII.

ACKNOWLEDGEMENTS

I gratefully acknowledge the permission of Her Majesty Queen Elizabeth II to republish extracts from Princess Victoria's private diary, previously uniquely published in J.F. Parsons' booklet, *Princess Victoria in Dorset*, written for Bournemouth Local Studies Publications.

Thomas Hardy's writings are out of copyright, but I am grateful to the Dorset County Museum, Dorchester, for permission to reproduce Thomas Hardy's own drawing of his birthplace at Bockhampton. I am also grateful to the Bournemouth Local Studies Group for permission to quote from the 1840 *Visitor's Guide to Bournemouth*.

I thank R.J. Saville, Chairman and Curator of Langton Matravers Local History and Preservation Society, for permission to use material from his booklet *A Langton Smuggler*, and also for his permission to reproduce his drawing of the lobster-pot. I am also grateful to the Trade Union Congress and Tolpuddle Martyrs' Trust, for permission to reproduce the drawing of the Tolpuddle Martyrs.

The drawing of the ram-headed god, Ammon, is by David Wilson, © Chambers Harrap Publishers Ltd.

The drawings of the 'Man with Toothache', the 'Man with Headache', Bow and Arrow Castle, the Monmouth Ash, and the Tower in Charborough Park are by Charles G. Harper.
The drawing of Wimborne Minster is by Joseph Pennell.
The drawing of Manor House and Bridge at Wool is by Charlotte Helen Mate.

All other illustrations are by myself.

David Hilliam, 2010

Other titles published by The History Press

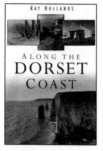

Along the Dorset Coast
Ray Hollands
978-07524-5185-5
Famous for its wonderful geological features such as Lulworth Cove, Chesil Beach and the Jurassic Coast, the unique atmosphere of the Dorset coastline is beautifully captured by Ray Hollands' eye-catching photography and informative history.

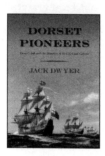

Dorset Pioneers
Jack Dwyer
978-07524-5346-0
This absorbing and beautifully written book traces the North American connection with Dorset characters such as Sir Walter Raleigh and the Tolpuddle Martyrs. For all those interested in Dorset and the history of the Americas, this is a must-have.

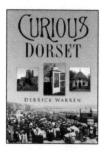

Curious Dorset
Derrick Warren
978-07509-3733-7
This book is a guide to about eighty of Dorset's remarkable and idiosyncratic sights, such as a clock tower with no clock, a duellist's tomb, a screaming skull and bits of old London. It makes fascinating reading for locals and visitors alike.

Visit our website and discover thousands of other History Press books.

www.thehistorypress.co.uk